Officious

Rise of the Busybody State

Officious

Rise of the Busybody State

Josie Appleton

Winchester, UK
Washington, USA

First published by Zero Books, 2016
Zero Books is an imprint of John Hunt Publishing Ltd., Laurel House, Station Approach,
Alresford, Hants, SO24 9JH, UK
office1@jhpbooks.net
www.johnhuntpublishing.com
www.zero-books.net

For distributor details and how to order please visit the 'Ordering' section on our website.

Text copyright: Josie Appleton 2015

ISBN: 978 1 78535 420 5
978 1 78535 421 2 (ebook)
Library of Congress Control Number: 2016937654

A CIP catalogue record for this book is available from the British Library.

Design: Stuart Davies

Printed and bound by CPI Group (UK) Ltd, Croydon, CR0 4YY, UK

We operate a distinctive and ethical publishing philosophy in all
areas of our business, from our global network of authors to
production and worldwide distribution.

CONTENTS

Acknowledgements

The ideas in this book were developed over a decade of work on the state hyperregulation of everyday life. I have drawn on conversations and email exchanges with people fined for an innocuous offence, or who opposed unreasonable regulations in their group or institution. I owe much to their detailed and perceptive accounts of events. Some of these individuals showed considerable courage in risking their reputations and positions to challenge officious rules, particularly Annabel Hayter and Jeremy Hummerstone.

The members of the Manifesto Club steering committee provided a welcome sounding board and source of ideas and examples.

Frank Furedi advised on several drafts of the text and informed the book's theoretical development. Stephen Davies recommended material on US criminal law and gave helpful suggestions on the text.

Douglas Lain and Ashley Frawley at Zero Books made valuable suggestions for additions and changes.

Friends and colleagues read through sections of the book, including Jonny Walker, Bruno Waterfield, Dolan Cummings, James Panton and Peter Lloyd.

Henri was my vital companion in writing.

All faults and errors are my own.

Introduction

In Anglo-Saxon countries there is now a new and distinctive form of state: the busybody state. This state is defined by an attachment to bureaucratic procedures for their own sake: the rule for the sake of a rule, the form for the sake of a form. Its insignias are the official badge, the policy, the code and the procedure. The logic of officious regulation is neither to represent an elite class interest, nor to serve the public, nor to organise social relations with the greatest efficiency as with classic bureaucracy, but rather to subject spontaneous areas of social life to procedures and rules.

The new state official and the new regulation are defined by their hostility to expressions of independence or subjectivity on the part of civil society. Where there are elements of independent social life – a busker in a street, a gathering on a beach – new officials will appear to tell them that they need a busking licence or that they are not allowed to drink there.

Thus the domain of civil society loses its independent and self-constituting quality. A public activity can be carried out only once it has been authorised, once you have been through the requisite procedures and obtained the necessary accreditation: a busking or leafleting licence, a child-protection training course, criminal-records vetting. Once it was assumed that everything was allowed unless explicitly prohibited; now it is more often assumed that everything is prohibited unless specifically allowed. The unauthorised action has become implicitly illegitimate, in some cases criminal.

This transformation has been rapid and thorough. A decade ago a political campaign group could set up a stall in a town or city centre and hand out leaflets, sell magazines or obtain signatures. Now they would be approached in a matter of minutes and asked to move on. The justification may vary: they may be told

1

that they require council approval for their leaflets or a charity-collection licence. They may be told that stalls and structures are prohibited, or that these structures require a risk assessment or that it is prohibited to sell unauthorised publications (or even to give them away for free). The specific form of paperwork demanded has a relatively arbitrary quality: what matters is that independent action is seen as illegitimate.

The busybody state is a concept that begins from people's everyday experience encountering the new official in public spaces. This everyday experience is embodied in a genre of YouTube videos in which cyclists, photographers or buskers are shown locked in a dispute with a badged official who is seeking to prevent them from continuing with their activity. The busybody's intervention appears as unnecessary and unreasonable; the busker's recalcitrant response as a defence of the essential legitimacy of free public action.

There is a widely recognised public discussion about 'meddling officials' and 'pointless red tape'. Although this is more associated with the right-wing popular press, it is present too on left-wing protest sites such as Indymedia, and the key elements would be recognised by anybody who attempts to act in public spaces or to take part in local activities or volunteering organisations.

This book begins from this everyday experience of conflict with one of these new officials, defining the unusual features of the busybody. It then proceeds to analyse the social structures and political logic which underlie this encounter.

The officious state is defined by distinct forms of legal regulation, surveillance and criminal punishment. The classical institutions of the bourgeois state have undergone substantial modification, with institutions tending to blur and merge into one another. Institutions lose their distinctive cultures and missions and become part of the amorphous realm of *officialdom*, which is defined not by a particular public mission but primarily by the extension of bureaucratic procedures over social life. It becomes increasingly difficult to distinguish some police officers from private security guards or council officials, as all move into the same zone of behaviour policing.

This new busybody state is not at all like a classic bureaucracy. Classic bureaucracy is defined by its strict regimentation of office and hierarchy, with each official a mere cog in a machine of social function. The new state is not so much a formal system of organisation, as a constantly mutating *formalism*, which is frequently disorganised in structure and arbitrary in content.

The officious state represents a new form of political authority. Every previous form of authority represented social interests in some way, some public constituency or political position which might be more or less popular or elitist. The distinct feature of officious regulation is its absolute detachment from all elements of social interest: it appears to come from nowhere and represent no-one. It represents the negation of social life and social meaning, and is as hostile to elite institutions as it is to working-class culture. The busybody doesn't represent this or that political camp, but rather the *third party* which rises up over established social forms. War veterans must queue up with political activists to gain their charity-collection licence; foxhunters are targeted as equally as football supporters. Officious authority rises up only in counter-position to the shady, dubious citizenry.

In a certain respect the new state approaches the pure essence of the state. Theorists including Marx, Engels and Lenin have located a defining feature of the state as lying in its 'special' quality: the fact that it is *raised above, separated out from* and *set against* social life.[1] Ultimately, the state is defined by the fact that it is not of social life, that it has special bodies and organs, special powers, which distinguish it from the citizenry.

The busybody state is grounded on nothing other than its distinction from the citizenry. The only thing commending a new official is his or her *possession of a badge*: it is the badge that endows them with their being, marking them out as special, not an ordinary person, and with powers over ordinary people. An official now is increasingly defined not by the particular institution they represent, nor their performance of a public function, but merely by their possession of a badge.

This state is the product of the peculiar political juncture at which we find ourselves, marked by the hollowing out of elite institutions and the erosion of social structures mediating the state and society. As a result, state structures are left unmoored, floating like an oil slick on top of society. They are left as sheer structures, sheer officialdom, facing the citizenry with the empty language of formalism and proceduralism. The officious state is ultimately the product of a social vacuum, a causative condition that it amplifies with every extension of regulation.

The rise of the officious state fundamentally transforms the lines of political conflict and allegiance. The divisions of left and right once represented the lines of class interest, with the state tending to mediate this conflict and represent the interests of the dominant class. Now the officious state has turned against social interests and relations of all kinds. As Marx wrote in his critique of Hegel's *Philosophy of Right*, the interest of the state has become a particular private purpose opposed to the other private purposes.[2] This raises the potential for a new political dividing line between the new officialdom and citizens, and an objective conflict of interest between parts of the state structure and civil society.

At the same time there is a new commonality of interest between varied groups who may previously have been in different political camps, such as foxhunters and football supporters, war veterans and political activists. When these very different groups enter into scuffles with official regulation they are all at base defending the same principle: the legitimacy of the domain of civil society and of their own free activity.

This context presents a new demand of social theory: to make conscious the commonality underlying apparently disparate conflicts between social groups and bureaucratic authority. This means a new politics defending the terrain of the unregulated or spontaneous social relations or activities that are initiated on their own account and maintained on their own terms. The task is to grasp the underlying dynamics of officious regulation, and to affirm life against the code, independence against incorporation, sincerity against the tick-box.

Photo used by permission of Jonny Walker

1

The new busybodies

The new busybodies can be found throughout social life. They are in the street in day-glo jackets, telling people that they should not play ball games or hand out leaflets. They are in institutions, enforcing criminal-records checks, drawing up safety signs or running diversity-awareness courses. They are in voluntary association or clubs, the child-protection officer or health-and-safety officer who fills in forms and invents new procedures with which everyone else must comply.

They have an identifiable manner. They are hawk-eyed, on the lookout for some minor infraction, for somebody who has used 'inappropriate' language or failed to draw up the requisite risk assessments and policy documents. They view the world through dubious and suspicious eyes: most people, they think, are up to no good. And when they discover a violation they draw themselves up: they have a *tone* which is talking down to you, but quite unlike the tone of those in positions of traditional moral authority. The tone of the busybody is sanctimonious – you have 'failed to comply' or committed 'unsafe practices' – but without the moral weight and grounding of a defined social position. They are uppity and hectoring, shrill with jabbing fingers. People who have been fined by a busybody often say that they felt humiliated, and indeed the exchange appears geared towards their humiliation.

The officious are quite distinct from public-service officials, whose raison d'être and authority is derived from the public: the things people want, the problems they face. Whereas public-service officials seek in various ways to meet public needs, the officious tend to obstruct people's activities, introducing rules that make life more difficult. Rather than representing the public will, officiousness seems rather to be the negative of the public will, not aiding and providing but restricting and stifling.

It is for this reason that these new officials are often rude and derisory. It is not uncommon for florescent-jacketed busybodies to swear at people or to be generally dismissive and disrespectful. One man was followed and called a 'pain in the ass' when he refused to pay a fine for litter he had not in fact dropped.[3] The officious ignore the usual dispensations accorded to the elderly or mothers with young children; they issue their fines and reprimands with an egalitarian disdain. Mothers have been fined when their child dropped a small food item,[4] elderly people for feeding the birds or unwittingly walking their dog in the wrong area.

Aside from this derisory manner, it is difficult to sum up the qualities of the officious in any positive terms. They have no particular beliefs, no ethical orientation. They are not religious or humanitarian, right or left, working-class or elite. They seem to come from nowhere and have no ties or loyalties to any particular social group.

It is easier to say what they are not. They are not like the traditional English police officer, representing interests of state and middle classes in facing down a riot or breaking a strike - while at the same time being the local bobby who gives directions and takes lost children home. Nor are they like the French gendarme, the representative of the state as military force, bound by *esprit de corps* and set against a potentially mutinous population to whom they relate as might an army of occupation. The officious do not seem to represent any particular social interests, either popular or interests of state and 'public order'.

Nor are busybodies like traditional bureaucrats. Bureaucrats, as Max Weber says, were defined by their 'precision, steadiness, and, above all, the speed of operations'.[5] Bureaucrats were loyal to their office, to the function dispatched without delay or favour, with a swift click-click. The drive of the bureaucrat came from the social necessity of his tasks, the standardised operations necessary for the workings of a modern society. The officious lack this social necessity and so lack the accompanying discipline and precision.

In fact the busybodies who patrol public spaces often wear ill-fitting jackets and seem to slouch. They have nothing like the policeman's hat or gendarme's cap, which in an earlier era were treated with such reverence that it was thought mutinous crowds would quail at the mere sight of them. The new officials tend to wear a black fleece or a fluorescent jacket, with a badge and perhaps a camera around their neck. This uniform is indicative. They are representing no particular authority, but are a sort of generic 'authorised person'. Their power is not in a symbol or uniform but in the badge they flash at you when issuing a fine. The florescent jacket has become the new 'authorised person' uniform, to the extent that it is used as a cover for heists and stunts.

The first Metropolitan police officers were distinguished from the lackadaisical parish constable by their 'perfect command of temper'. In joining the police, a 'wild young fellow' became 'a machine, moving, thinking and acting only as his instruction book directs': 'an institution rather than a man'.[6] The individual became part of a bureaucratic machine, subject to strict orders and lines of command, every morning lined up and given their brief.

By contrast the new officials' behaviour can be random and unpredictable. They lose their cool and shout at people, or get into an argument, trying it on, then walk off. They seem alternately coasting around doing nothing then haranguing people and bothering them. You don't know what they are going to do next. Because there is no particular professional brief, they seem to pick on the things that annoy them personally or on people to whom they have taken a dislike.

The officious have no devotion to office as such: they are

generally indifferent to or set against the institution of which they are part. There is a trans-institutional culture of officiousness, which traverses institutions as different as schools, councils, hospitals and art galleries. Very different sectional interests produce day-glo busybodies, indistinguishable except by close examination of their badge: they could be from private companies, councils or the police. These officials talk the same language and can move easily between jobs in different sectors. They often believe that their institution is beset with a host of problems, whether that is racism, sexism, environmentally unfriendly or 'unsafe' habits, and the institution is equally the target for their interventions as is the general public.

At base, these officials' only positive allegiance is to the *mechanisms of officialdom*; their only belief is in the inherent virtues of regulation. The objects of their faith are the database, the form, the code; these forms of bureaucratic procedure are attributed with a fetishistic power. They demand that every organisation has 'policies in place', which is seen as a guarantee of safety and right conduct, regardless of what the policy actually says. 'Procedures' are seen as in themselves capable of warding off evil, and if people have complied with the official code then their action is judged 'safe', while the lack of a policy, or deviation from it ('non-compliance') is seen as inherently foolhardy and dangerous.

Officious jobs

There are officious job positions within every institution. Some purportedly deal with safety or public protection, such as health-and-safety officer, safer-travel coordinator, child-protection trainer, neighbourhood wardens, community-support officers. Others with equality: diversity officer, access or social-inclusion officer. Others with health or environmental wellbeing: alcohol-policy officer, smoking-cessation adviser, healthy-eating officer, climate-change officer, energy-efficiency officer, recycling coordinator, environmental-enforcement officer, smoke-free officer. Finally, with institutional management: change manager, human-resources manager, strategic-development officer, quality-assurance officer, compliance officer.

If these were public-service jobs, each role would relate to a very distinct public need: one would empty bins, another would clean rivers or investigate sex-abuse allegations. The job would respond to a specific public need for rubbish disposal, a clean environment or the prosecution of crime, and seek that specific useful end.

There is a general recognition that officious jobs lack this useful or productive function. Some have called them 'non-jobs'[7], which are seen as 'useless' and 'money-wasting', obsessed with 'jargon' and 'pointless rules'.

This presentation captures an aspect of truth, but officious jobs are not just creative ways of burning money. They have a logic and perform a function (albeit not a useful one). Their purported function related to sex offences or the environment is a mere garb, because in substance they all have the same content and role: to extend regulation over social life. The officious intervention transforms unregulated life into regulated life; it colonises civil society with standardised forms of thought and behaviour.

Rather than starting from the position of a public need, these officials start from the position of problematic public behaviours, such as people leaving lights on, failing to recycle correctly, organising events without the latest safety guidance, drinking too much, smoking or eating unhealthy foods. The job is not related to a need or a public demand but to an identified problem with the things people are doing. Officious action does not serve but instead *acts upon* the public.

The role of officious jobs is generally to carry out 'interventions' in order to encourage 'safer' or more 'appropriate' behaviours. This doesn't mean behaviour that is actually safer or more considerate of others; instead it means more regulated behaviour, which conforms to standards of etiquette or recommended guidelines. The officious aim is to encourage people to follow recommended codes or procedures: to put rubbish items in the correct bin, to use accepted words, fill in the requisite forms or eat the recommended portions of fruit and vegetables. The end is the suppression of free thought and action and the regimentation of conduct.

Institutions have a strand of officious jobs which run relatively independently of and indeed contrary to the rest of the institution. Those seeking to perform a more traditional public-service role find themselves in conflict with the more officious layers of activity. In rubbish-collection services, for example, there are bin men who perform a classic public-service role and useful task. Within the same department there is a layer of officious people with a quite different role: going from door to door issuing reprimands and fines, telling people off for having over-filled the bin, put the bin in the wrong place or placed items in the wrong bin. (These two different strands were shown very clearly in the Cutting Edge documentary *Revenge of the Bin Men*).

While bin men aim to fulfil the public need for waste collection as quickly and simply as possible, the clipboard officials are constantly frustrating the process, inventing new bins and new sorting rules, and increasingly sophisticated surveillance methods to catch people who are failing to comply with their rules. They get exercised if somebody has left their bin lid open by an inch or has put a recyclable item in their regular rubbish.

These jobs work in the opposite directions: the bin men to take bins away, the officious to view the surveillance cameras placed in bins, or to empty out rubbish bags in search of illegitimate items which are then bagged or photographed as evidence of noncompliance. One woman in Westminster was fined for putting a single work bank statement in her domestic rubbish, after the council officer who examined the contents of her bin classed this as 'commercial waste'.[8] Capital expenditure is also at odds, with a new van or street cleaner which would aid rubbish collection pitted against more enforcement wardens or surveillance equipment to aid officious functions.

A similar division of function can be found in other institutions and professions. Local authority health-and-safety departments include officers who enforce hygiene standards in restaurants or investigate factories where there have been accidents. Here the aim is to enforce necessary standards for public protection: washed hands, clean surfaces, machines with adequate guards, restrictions on working hours. In these cases the regulations have a clear raison d'être, protecting the public from hazards over which they have little control. In the same department, however, there are positions which serve not to aid but to obstruct. It is these officials who preoccupy themselves banning pancake races or bonfires, who say that the cakes at the village fete cannot be homemade and that the fete needs a fire exit. They put up signs reading 'caution steps' and demand that every activity be risk assessed and covered with public liability insurance.

The logic of these jobs works in opposite directions: one protects the public, the other is set against the public, preventing people from doing the things they want to do. One makes life easier, the other harder.

We must emphasise that officious health and safety does little to achieve substantial health and safety (ditto environmental protection, child protection). This can be seen by the distorted nature of officious health-and-safety interventions, which are often blithely indifferent to genuine hazards. When a council tenant in Brighton put up Christmas lights on his balcony, the council told him to take them down because they had not been safety checked by an electrician. The council had also told residents that their doormats were dangerous and should be removed from corridors. Yet at the same time (as the head of the tenants' association pointed out) there were chunks of cracked concrete falling off the building and two-foot icicles hanging from the balconies, which threatened to impale those on the balconies below.[9] The council was uninterested in this actual threat to life and limb; for it, public initiative was the hazard.

Officious regulation does not solve a problem, but makes a problem out of the things people are doing, and therefore restricts, incorporates social life within its domain and subjects pockets of spontaneity to formalised systems of comportment.

The rise of the officious in institutions

Over time, the officious strands have grown as a portion of an institution. Within council environmental departments the numbers of wardens issuing fines for minor misdemeanours start to rival those performing a useful waste-collection function. There are more people involved in vetting volunteers and running child-protection training courses than there are working in child protection proper, investigating abuse allegations or prosecuting abuse cases. The police child-protection department is the poor cousin of criminal investigation: one former police chief complained that there were more officers in her force carrying out criminal-records checks than there were investigating or prosecuting child-abuse cases.[10]

The numbers are stark: in England and Wales there are 120,000 serving police constables and sergeants. There are around the same number of busybodies: some 10,000 council wardens, 13,000 police community-support officers, over 2000 'accredited persons' (private employees given police powers) and 100,000 private security guards. And because these officious wardens may have less to do, you are more likely to meet one of these than you are a police officer. The officious officer is becoming the predominant presence in public space.

Within universities there is a growing dominance of the human-resources or management sector who play an increasingly prominent role in academic life, even issuing instructions for the names of courses or procedures for the marking of papers. Twenty years ago universities either had no managers or nobody knew who they were; now 'management' send out a constant stream of missives on how this or that ought to be done.

It is notable that when under financial pressure, institutions often strengthen their officious layers and cut their substantial public-service sections. After budget cuts, many London councils closed old people's homes and other services, but at the same time they expanded their CCTV programmes.[11] They cut rubbish collection, while increasing litter wardens going out to fine people. It is the officious (and useless) aspect of their work that appears essential, while the substantial public service appears dispensable.

The reason for this is that officious forms of thought and practice have become the primary basis for institutional and professional authority. It is through these procedures that institutions justify themselves and mark out their boundaries. The officious procedure increasingly marks the gateway to an institution: when you enter the door you are asked for your ID or subjected to a bag search. The bag search replaces the welcome at the door. When you offer to volunteer your first action is to fill in a police check form. Similarly, the announcement about fire-escape procedure has become the standard introduction to public meetings or even to events such as weddings or christenings. The officious procedure becomes the authoritative basis of an institution, the way it introduces itself and the point from which it commands.

There are cases of head teachers going to the wall to enforce a photography ban in school plays, or bans on cartwheels, chocolate bars or orange juice. The persistence with which they stand by the issue – their resolute facing down of protesting parents as if in battle fatigues – indicates that this procedure has become the primary grounding of their professional authority.[12] The question of the restriction of parent photography becomes the primary issue on which the authority of the school is staked.

Old ways of persuading or commanding have lost their power. Doctors have been prohibited from telling patients that they are fat[13] yet at the same time overweight patients in Wales can be compelled to go on obesity courses.[14] Direct words from a professional are superseded by the course run by a healthy-eating adviser. Similarly, badly behaving children are faced not with a telling off but with a swathe of officious procedures: fines for truancy, good-behaviour contracts, anti-social behaviour orders, while their parents are issued with parenting contracts and orders. As the figures of social authority have waned, officious authorities take their place and seek to discipline through sheer weight of paperwork.

Officious positions such as the child-protection or health-and-safety officer seem to bypass the normal hierarchy of political or professional authority within an institution. They are in effect outside of the normal chain of command; they have an authority which trumps the rest. They are in a position to criticise anyone – even the head of the institution or the Archbishop of Canterbury himself – for behaving 'inappropriately' or failing to implement the required procedures or checks.

The health-and-safety or child-protection officer is given the run of institutions. In the Church of England, for example, child-safeguarding officers go around church volunteer groups submitting elderly volunteers to criminal-records checks. If these volunteers refuse (protesting that they have been in the church for decades and should be trusted) they are told: 'fine, don't do it; but don't come to church'.[15] People's membership of the church is henceforth conditional upon submitting to officious procedures. The safeguarding officer holds the church keys, summarily dismissing those who have been loyal church members for 50 years or more.

Over time, officious positions become more attractive than public-service jobs. In politics, becoming a minister is increasingly unattractive: a better position is chairman of a select committee which means you can haul other people in and give them a going over. The doers are on the wane; to do things exposes you to flack. The rising stars are the interrogators, investigators, the prodders and pokers, the positions of third-party authorities who oversee and judge others. Within an institution the public-service parts increasingly start to resemble the officious parts, as public servants are pressured down these new lines of activity whether they like it or not.

Now to examine the mindset of the officious. The officious negativity towards the public can be broken down into two elements: first, vindictiveness, an appearance of being out to get people; and second, suspicion and bad faith.

Vindictiveness and vendettas

The new officials seem driven to punish or to incriminate people, often for innocuous or obscure reasons. Within institutions the officious collect dossiers on their colleagues. The diversity officer listens carefully to conversations, on the lookout for any language which suggests discriminatory attitudes or which could be interpreted as such. The safeguarding officer in the Scouts or church seems driven to incriminate other volunteers, reporting an inappropriate word or gesture (calling a girl 'love', or putting an arm around an upset child). One Scout leader was reported by his safeguarding officer for saying that condoms could be used as an emergency water carrier, a piece of advice that is in fact in the Scout handbook.[16]

These dossiers generally don't deal with criminal or genuinely harmful behaviour. Instead, it is a question of using the wrong words or failing to moderate tone or gesture in the required manner. It is *spontaneity* that is being punished – that natural enemy of all things officious. The individuals who become the target of dossiers are often those of a previous generation, who are not sufficiently restrained and joke around or are open or straight-talking. The offence is merely to behave in a spontaneous or natural manner, without stopping and thinking about how a gesture could *look* to someone who wanted to read the worst into it.[17]

The other target of vendettas is *insubordination*: the fact that somebody refuses to undergo a criminal-records check, for example, or challenges a photo ban or other safety rules. A person's irreverence or refusal to go along with 'requirements' marks them out for attention and for the collecting of evidence against them. Safeguarding officers collect evidence of their non-compliance, including irreverent comments made in private conversations or emails. One priest had a 100-page dossier prepared against him by the diocese safeguarding officer, including critical comments he had made in the church newsletter about safety signs in his church.[18] He was reported for the offence of having 'persistently or recklessly failed to comply with the safeguarding policies and procedures of the organisation'.

Yellow-jacketed busybodies in public spaces exhibit a similar drive to get people, hiding in bushes[19] or in crowds and leaping out when an elderly lady drops a cigarette butt or a dog walker strays into the wrong area. When they spot someone committing a misdemeanour they rush over, full of haughty indignation. Wardens have been witnessed running after people, chasing them into shops and pulling them out again,[20] laughing when someone has been successfully fined.[21]

A policeman shows no similar glee at having caught a criminal: he has merely dispatched his office. He doesn't leap about or laugh when he issues a fine.

For the officious officer, the act of punishment of another individual is the realisation of their professional position, and is sought regardless of whether the punishment has basis or not. They are like bloodhounds on the trail and continue the pursuit, snapping at the heels and flanks until their target falls.

In every case they are demanding that someone *submits*, which may mean an apology, a resignation, leaving an area or stopping an activity, or paying a fine. These moments of submission seem to be sought as an end in themselves, and are pursued almost in deliberate indifference to the fact that the accusation is unjustified: when it is very clear that somebody was not actually being sexist or that they didn't know the park was a no-dog zone.

The reason for this is not that the new officials are particularly vindictive in character. Rather, it is the consequence of the position they occupy, the fact that they have no public duty or role and represent nothing beyond themselves. Their raison d'être is therefore a negative one, set against and undermining others. This orientation is encouraged by incentives or expectations that they will issue large numbers of fines or report large numbers of incidents. A lack of reported incidents or fines would indicate that they are not doing their job properly.

New officials tend to concentrate on the most minor issues (it is a common public complaint that they 'pick on easy targets'). Their remit is not that of substantial violations – of assault or abuse or theft – but of nit-picking and etiquette, matters of non-compliance with this or that rule which you may or may not have heard of. The criminal individual is not as compelling a target as essentially innocent people who have committed an indiscretion. Their interest in an issue runs in inverse proportion to its real public importance.

The officious act of state intervention is becoming its own drive and source of satisfaction, without the necessity of law and order or public-service interventions. When there is a criminal act the act of intervention is dictated by the event: the victim must be taken to hospital, the criminal pursued, evidence gathered, a prosecution mounted. The violation dictates the form and structure of the response. The officious sanction tends towards a pure and unjustified intervention, which is most freely pursued where there is no actual problem there at all.

Bad faith and suspicion

Officious suspicion is a universal bearing, a general manner of looking at the world and relating to others. A grandmother offering to listen to reading at her grandchild's school is asked to undergo criminal-records checks to prove she is not a sex offender. Babies' milk must be tasted at airports to show that it is not a liquid bomb.

Sometimes these requests are justified on practical grounds, albeit with intellectual contortions. One child-protection officer justified nativity photo bans (preventing parents taking photos of their children dressed as wise men or angels) on the basis that a child's face 'could be cut out and stuck on the photo of a naked child's body'.[22] However, in most cases the request is not a sincerely held belief about somebody, nor a practically justified measure, but instead is a ritual, a way of relating which is completely undiscerning. If you asked the official, do you really think this grandmother could be a paedophile, or the baby milk a bomb, they would think 'no', but they would say, 'it doesn't matter, everybody has to comply with these procedures'.

The bearing of universal bad faith is nothing personal. To protest is to take it personally. When a young American man refused to go through a naked body scanner, and then refused an intimate body search that would go 'right to the top' of his thigh, the security guard told him: 'Everybody has submitted themselves [to these checks]. I have submitted myself.'[23] And indeed, universal suspicion becomes a kind of ethic to which people are scrupulous about not making exceptions.

The officious eye is the third eye of constant suspicion, which presides over interactions and sees them in the worst possible light. One should act to assuage this third party; you should avoid any actions which 'could be misinterpreted'. The question is not what you meant, nor what the other person understood by your actions, but whether your actions 'could be misinterpreted'. Therefore one should act to assuage this figure of bad faith – to withdraw your hand, and be careful with your language – even while you and they know that their suspicion is unfounded and a *mis*-interpretation.

It is unusual for suspicion to be directed at so wide a frame. Historically, suspicion tended to be directed at certain outsider groups (suspected witches, homosexuals, Jews) who were seen as the receptacles of destabilising or contaminating forces. The fantastical scenarios of moral panics represented a negation of majority values: the witches' night of the Sabbath, fornicating with the devil and boiling babies, was to its last detail the antithesis of the Christian Sabbath. In moral panics the figure of suspicion was a specific minority, and the fearful fantasies derived from the reference point of majority values, which sought to expel the other and reground themselves.

The role of generalised officious suspicion is to reaffirm officious authority. Social life is seen as terroristic, paedophilic, shady, suspicious; against this officiousness rises up with the power of cleansing and with its touch declares people clean and safe. Once someone has submitted to a search or been vetted then they are declared clean, safe, trustworthy. The authority of suspicious procedures is not based on their effectiveness, but merely on their *detachment* from shady and suspicious social life, that they are raised above and set against social life. The universal and blanket suspicion of social life goes along with a universal and blanket faith in bureaucratic procedures.

The war on civil society

Although we have examined the mindset and psychology of these new officials, this is not ultimately a question of character or psychology. This is not a question of the 'meddling' characters of certain individuals, but the socio-structural position they occupy which is forging of character and conduct. Structurally, officious institutions are hostile towards and turned against civil society as a whole.

It is notable that officious rules do not target a particular class or group, but fall equally upon everyone: skateboarding children, political activists handing out leaflets, friends having a drink in the park. The officious disdain towards the public is not a snobbery or class alliance, but a general bearing towards the population at large.

So we find that new regulations target people from every class and group. Italian mayors brought through a series of bans which fell on all parts of society without distinction. They banned 'very short' skirts, which targeted liberated young women; lying down on benches and ambulant sellers, which targeted immigrants; and ball games and climbing trees, which targeted children.[24]

Past forms of regulation tended to be founded in the interests of a particular class. In the 19th century the British elite banned cock-fighting and bear-baiting, and regulated taverns, dances and working-class gambling – but left elite habits untouched, so that private clubs were left free to drink and gamble as they pleased and the aristocracy continued to chase foxes across the countryside. Now the upper classes are subjected to the rule of the bureaucrats as much as anyone else: their private clubs are not allowed smoking rooms, foxhunting has also been banned, and they must also line up for their police checks and searches.

The officious rule is turned not against a particular group, and it expresses no alliance with any social interest or moral position. The target is social life in toto.

Specifically, the target of the officious rule is *unregulated life*, anything that people have done or chosen for themselves using their own judgement or initiative, or any relationship based on spontaneity and mutual trust.

For example, child-protection regulation targets the 'relationship of trust',[25] which is seen as the site of potential abuse and therefore as requiring central state vetting and regulation. Inherent elements of closeness or privacy are seen as 'risky': a closed door, driving a child home, any friendship or trust between an adult and a child. It is the unregulated human relationship, and not actual or potentially abusive behaviour, which is the target for regulation.

Pockets of spontaneity attract the officious like moths to a candle. The areas of life which were previously freest of regulation have become the particular focus for new rules.

The English pub was traditionally a semi-autonomous sphere, with frosted glass and backrooms where the landlord held sway and police could enter only in the direst of emergencies. This has now become one of the most regulated spheres, with requirements for bag searches, ID scans and restrictions on certain cocktail names and happy hours. The very site of freedom becomes a particular target of officiousness.

Similarly, the beach was traditionally a space of semi-wilderness, independent from the conventions of the town. It was acceptable to do things on beaches that would not be allowed in a park: petting, nudity, sleeping in public. The threshold of the beach was a line of freedom, a release from social control. Now the beach has become the particular target for rules and regulations, with bans in various places on: ball games, beach tents, kites, barbecues, smoking and drinking, dog-walking, building sandcastles, surfing. It is the very freedom of the beach which marks it out for special attention, special bans (smoking is banned on the beach but not in the street) and special patrols by officials to confiscate alcohol or issue reprimands.

For the first time in history, this is not a case of one class set against another, but of officiousness against civil society. It is no longer the elite versus the working classes but the officious against free social life itself.

Summary: officious authority

Officious authority is a completely new kind of authority. It is authority which is entirely negative, based on a negation of all other forms of social authority, both popular and elite, civic and institutional. Officious authority is not founded on its own qualities, its own competence or representative power, but only on the presumed incompetence and illegitimacy of others.

Every previous ideology was somehow grounded in some social group, some interest or ethic, which provided its drive and orientation. A claim to authority could be based upon personal qualities (such as in Homer, that somebody is the fastest or strongest) or the interests or ethic that one represents.[26] Officiousness has no such grounding: it is supremely asocial, estranged from social life and set against it.

It is also not even grounded in the self-interest or self-seeking of a clique. The officious are not a classic parasitic class, like an aristocracy or a political clique lustily seeking their own benefits and enrichment at the expense of others. They are not strongmen or Machiavellian types driven by their own positive interests, however selfish and partial these may be.

Officious authority lords it over others, but is also self-denying. This is not a party – a party with interests, aims and desires – but merely the 'third party', the policers, watchers, adjudicators of the actions of others. These new officials do not seek their own enrichment or build vanity projects. They are not asserting themselves but are merely the impassive ciphers through which officious rules flow.

Hence the way in which everyone presents officious rules as

something beyond their authorship or control. The compliance officer might say that the rules are 'necessary to comply with health and safety obligations', but the health-and-safety officer says that they are actually because of EU or data-protection law, and so the chain goes on. These rules are everywhere but nobody has written them, apparently, and nobody will speak for them. They seem to breed and mutate of their own account, as one version of 'best practice' transforms into another.

At base, officiousness represents the negation of free will. This is the meaning of the phrase 'procedures must be followed': it means that action must not be chosen but must follow the abstract, impersonal rule, whose sole commendation is its restriction on free thought and action. The sole commendation of officiousness is that it is restricted, that it is not free.

In a similar way, the sole commendation of an officious person is that they are not an ordinary citizen, that they are raised above and defined against the citizenry at large. They have no positive qualities or allegiances to commend them. They are only the non-citizen, claiming their authority on the basis of their separation from the shady, illegitimate mass of people of all classes. Their sole grounding is that they have some form of *badge*, some title (that they are some kind of 'officer'), which marks them out as separate from the public.

This is indicated by the 'accredited persons scheme', which gives police powers to private individuals such as security guards and the employees of transport companies. An 'accredited person' is not a police officer, the trained and moulded representative of state authority; nor are they just a person. This individual is the person who has been plucked from the crowd and given a badge, *accredited*, given powers over people and thus endowed with special capacities.

These badges are given out in an off-hand manner, without a great deal of attention as to whom police authorities are endowing with coercive powers. Only around 20 percent of police authorities keep accounts of how many fines these individuals have given out and they do not themselves investigate complaints about an accredited person's behaviour.[27] The accredited person's only training could be a five-day course supplied by a private company. What seems important is not the person's discipline or their accountability to policy or lines of command but the sheer fact of their *accreditation*, the badge marking them out as special.

This is a capacity based only on the imagined incapacity of others. The badged busybody gains his authority not from his own capacities but from the presumed incapability and shadiness of the citizen.

The Scottish government is appointing a 'named person' for every child from birth, who will be responsible for dealing with general concerns about the child's wellbeing. The state has effectively appointed shadow parents; the sole commendation of these shadow parents is that they are *named*, that they have been formally appointed and are from outside the family. This named person could be a child professional (a teacher or social worker) but their authority is grounded not on their professional expertise but only on their naming by the state, the fact that they have been tapped on the shoulder and appointed.

Perversely, real parents – who organise their lives around raising their children, day in and day out – are seen as unreliable judges of their best interests, while this randomly appointed state parent (who could, after all, be anyone) is endowed with great insight.

We are seeing a new deification of the mechanisms of bureaucracy and its representatives, only because they are *not free*, based on the restriction of free thought and will; and because they are *not of social life*, but estranged from and set against it.

This essentially negative basis gives the category of the busybody an evanescent and fluid quality. It is produced as a negation of existing arrangements, existing parties, and so lacks substantial definition of its own. It is always susceptible to itself being negated, to being itself declared a party and being superseded by another authority presuming to stand in judgement of *it*. And so systems of checking often lead to further checks of the checks, internal audits lead to external audits, audits of the audits, and so on, as the third parties breed one over another.[28]

2

Officiousness in context

The historical basis of bureaucracy

Bureaucratic forms have existed since ancient Egypt, and have two essential elements at their base. The first is the performance of some complex or large-scale public function, some objective purposes: the distribution of Nile waters in Egypt, the canals of Mesopotamia; or in modern times public roads, waterways and railroads.

The second feature is that these public functions are performed by special bodies, separated out from the population at large and possessing coercive powers over them. The official is not a mere public representative: they possess a set of powers and attributes that mark their difference from the ordinary citizen. Karl Marx described the offence of insulting an official in Prussia: 'Prussian despotism... confronts me with an official who is a superior, sanctified being. His character as an official is inter-woven into him like the consecration in a Catholic priest... Offending such a priest... remains a religious profanation.'[29]

The first feature of bureaucracy arises out of public need; the second arises out of conflicting social relations. It is with the emergence of class divisions that bureaucratic forms first appear, arising over conflicting social relations. Friedrich Engels highlights the development of the state army in ancient Greece, whereby the spontaneously assembled people as armed force was replaced by a separate body with its own lines of command: 'the institution of a *public force*... is no longer immediately identical with the people's organisation of themselves as an armed power... The officials now stand, as organs of society, *above society*.'[30] The public force was not now controlled by the people as a whole, and indeed could be used against them when occasion demanded (as in Sparta, where instruments of state were turned in continual warfare against the helot slave class).

Bureaucratic forms both mediate a social contradiction – it is an impartial third form, neither patricians nor plebs, aristocracy nor bourgeoisie – and at the same time acts in the interest of the dominant class. This was the case not only in Sparta but also in modern times. Even Max Weber noted that the propertyless did not stand to gain much from the legal system and that by and large bureaucracies acted in the interests of the propertied.

There is a further reason why bourgeois interests are manifested in a system of impersonal and detached institutions, raised above and set apart from particular interests. This reason is grounded in contradictions within the bourgeois class itself. Hegel's *Philosophy of Right* views the civil service as the 'universal class', which transcends and unites the particular interests of civil society. In civil society individuals exist as competing private interests, each set against the others; the universal function of seeking the public benefit is performed by a separate body insulated from these private interests. Hegel argued that civil society is not capable of realising the universal good spontaneously or directly; public functions are carried out with an element of coercion in order to 'prevail against' the solipsism of private interests.

In summary: classic bureaucratic forms perform public functions, mediate contradictory social relations, and represent the interests of the governing class. The balance of these different roles at any point will depend on the balance of social interests.

Bureaucratic autonomy

In certain periods, the bureaucracy has assumed a more independent and parasitic function in relation to society, no longer serving social interests but instead serving itself.

This was Marx's early view of bureaucracy in his youthful critique of Hegel's *Philosophy of Right*: the state as a private purpose set against other private purposes. Later he saw bureaucracy as defending the interests of the propertied, but argued that under certain conditions it could develop a relative autonomy from social interests, such as in absolutist France and Prussia or Bonapartism in 19th-century France.

In these cases the bureaucracy took an independent class-like form, subordinating other social interests to itself. Under the French *ancien regime* the burgeoning bureaucracy became the pole of attraction for bourgeois groups, who spent their fortunes on the purchase of state office. They would risk anything, even ruin, for the chance of obtaining a good position.[31] These state offices meant the discharge of a public function, such as administration of justice or collecting taxes, but they also endowed the holder with noble title. At a time when feudal status relations were eroding in society they took on a new artificial life in the realm of the state. The state became a block on emergent social forms, an 'appalling parasitic body, which enmeshes the body of French society and chokes all its pores'.[32]

Marx and Engels explained these periods of bureaucratic autonomy as the result of the stalemate of class interests – between the bourgeoisie and nobility for the absolutist state, and the bourgeoisie and proletariat for the Bonapartist state. Each of these social groups had interests which, when generalised, would imply a particular social system and logic of social organisation. In the conditions of temporary stalemate the instruments for the organisation of society (lying in the hands of the monarch or emperor) acquired a peculiar independence and power.

There are other circumstances in which bureaucracies have assumed an autonomous and self-interested role. One, in late Rome, is after the wholesale decay of the ruling class and the predominance of a general condition of social fragmentation. Hal Draper notes that by 300AD the Roman state's function shifted from preserving social order to 'replacing the organiser-classes of disintegrating civil society with its own cadres and mechanisms'. When 'a whole civil society disintegrates' the state structure supplants society and subordinates everything to itself:

> the autonomised state becomes the residual legatee of society for a historical period. The political institutionalization of force, the state, infuses all the processes of society and subordinates everything to itself; the political and economic institutions fuse. The state is no longer simply a superstructure; it has swallowed up all of society.[33]

The old patrician class dumped property and sold land, anything to escape the grasping extortion of the bureaucratic infrastructure which, released from serving social interests, was sucking the population dry.

Bureaucracy also achieved a peculiar autonomy in the Soviet Union under Stalin, where bureaucratic organs were directly politicised and wielded by a class of administrators who occupied a different world to the rest of the population, with separate neighbourhoods, special shops and restaurants. The market economy and intermediate institutions had been destroyed or suspended, so the single element of direction was the bureaucratic machine. Every significant event was the result of three-line orders issued from governing bureaucratic organs: that so many shoes be produced in this factory, that another person be appointed director of the Institute of Science, that a general be given a particular honour. This was a control bureaucracy possessing a complete 'monopoly of decision'.[34]

Bureaucrats formed a directly exploiting class, the *nomenklatura*, which wielded state machinery to skim off the wealth of society. Official position was directly equated with economic status and with a relationship of economic exploitation. One émigré commented that he was surprised in the West to see that public positions did not automatically enrich a person and that there was no sharp economic dividing line between those within the state structure and those without.[35]

Is officiousness a bureaucracy?

Classic bureaucracies have always had a certain insulation from the public and a certain hostility towards public opinion (embodied in traditions such as the 'office secret', protecting official business from public view) but these were mechanisms for shielding the world of officialdom from certain pressures, the better to enact systems representing other interests.

The officious bureaucracy is quite different. The officious individual is not protecting his own world; he is not caught up in intricate systems of functions and duties, exams and promotions. The whole world of bureaucratic status – the concern with the art of administration, the training in technique, the intricate distinctions of grade of job which are marked out as a career path of increasing prestige on which the bureaucrat's eyes are fixed – all this is not the world of the busybody.

At base, the officious state is not an organised construction, it is not a *system*, with each official as a mere cog in the finely whirring mechanism. The officious state has entirely abandoned the bureaucratic disciplines of jurisprudence and administration. Max Weber's description of bureaucratic organisation is that of regulating each matter 'abstractly', leaving nothing to individual decisions case by case.[36] Bureaucracy is a calculating, abstracting machine, which divides social function up into a pyramid of distinct spheres. Its watchwords are: precision, stability, discipline, reliability. The official shows 'painstaking obedience' within his 'sphere of action'. To each official a domain. The official expresses nothing of himself but is determined by the logic of the system; he is impersonality incarnate.

By comparison, the officious state is a disorganised, fluid, unpredictable, frequently dysfunctional construction. There are similar ways of talking and working, with common policies and language and forms of 'best practice', but this is a *similarity*, a similarity of position and perspective and a similar openness to the adoption of formulaic words. It is not an *inner relation*, based on an organised system where each individual is allotted a distinct role and subject to lines of command.

In fact, the development of the officious state can be seen as a process of *debureaucratisation*, as the unravelling of classic bureaucratic machines. When police forces hand out fining powers to civilian or private security organisations these new officials are released from lines of control and command. They are not part of an institutional structure governing the exercise of power; they are freelancers and free agents, undercutting traditional bureaucratic systems of law and order. They act case-by-case, almost without oversight or strictures. Their incentives are often private, such as gaining commission for each fine issued. They are in fact the anathema of bureaucracy proper, which is why these new officials have been firmly opposed by police unions and magistrate associations.

The forms of the officious state do not result from the undisciplined character of officials, but from the particular nature of state authority at the present time. The essence of the officious state is the autonomous bureaucratic *mechanism*, detached from social rationale and therefore from systemic features. It is bureaucracy reduced to an instrument, a technique. It is not a social form but an autonomous *formalism*, the multiplication of rules and forms of third-party authority as an end in itself.

Officiousness is state-*like* conduct, law-like rules. It is the trope of law, the trope of officialdom. It is the *outer form* of bureaucracy – the appearance of calculation and of rule-like conduct – adopted as clothing, behind which lie a variety of private or personal interests, or indeed no interests at all. It is the bureaucratic process as a performance.

When bureaucratic mechanisms are detached from their roots in a system, they can be adopted by a variety of different pressures and interests. The officious role can be played by anyone; it is a position remarkably open to the free play of subjectivity. The new officials are playing at being official and there is an openness for others to do the same. There is a competition in public debate to play the officious part, to draw yourself up and say that you find your opponent's conduct 'disappointing' or 'inappropriate'. Officiousness is therefore inherently fluid: a third party can be called into question and made a party, over whom others stand in judgement, or a party can rise up to play the third party.

In sum, we can see the officious state both as the logical conclusion of the bureaucratic form – taking the separation and formalism of bureaucracy to a logical extreme – while at the same time violating the essence of bureaucracy as a system. The officious state is a development out of the bureaucratic system of organisation, and expresses certain essential features of the capitalist state in an accentuated form. Yet these features appear as a shell, shorn of their social or class content. The mechanisms of bureaucracy reproduce themselves, in isolation from and defiance of social forms, lacking both logic and reality.

The officious state is the product of a society in which social contradictions continue – conflicts between the state and society, between individuals in society – but they are no longer organised in any systematic manner. The officious mechanism provides a mediation of social conflict where this remains trapped in the realm of the immediate and subjective.

3

Structure and origins of the officious state

The causes of the officious state

The sociological basis of the officious state is, first and foremost, the collapse of different forms of social regulation, both elite and popular. Officiousness is produced by conditions of social vacuum and absence. It is only with the waning of positive ideologies and social forms that officiousness comes to the fore as an organising dynamic.

So long as there are positive social forms, these will rule and keep officiousness on the sidelines, restricted to the tut-tutters and curtain twitchers at the margins of life. A positive trumps a negative; social content trumps absence. It is the decline of other forms of social authority which explains why the officious have risen to the top of institutions.

We can divide sociological changes into the following areas: 1. elite institutions, such as the professions, civil service, City, government; 2. mass institutions such as political parties and unions, which connected public and state; and 3. forms of association in civil society, such as sports groups, charities, social clubs, which were self-regulating and independent of the state.

In England, these different elements of social life were peculiarly well-developed and based on informal self-regulation. Elite institutions were unusually independent and self-regulating, relying as much as on club culture and agreements between 'decent chaps' as on formal codes or regulation. The political party structure was unusually stable and all-encompassing, running from parliament down to Conservative associations in the gardens of middle England and smoky Labour clubs in Northern towns. Finally, civic life was notably independent of officialdom: both working and middle-class neighbourhoods had networks of associations (sporting, charitable, social) which were organised without formal registration or contact with state authority.

These three dimensions of social life underwent a simultaneous and interconnected crisis, beginning in the 80s and completing by the early 20th century. The erosion of these three dimensions of social life occurred partly through an internal hollowing out, and partly through the initiative of specific government reforms which were carried out with an unusual completeness and reforming zeal – such as Thatcher's march through the institutions, privatisation and the attack on the unions, and the creation of new forms of central state regulation.

By the early 2000s, society was no longer organised in blocks of social interests. The social and cultural had receded: internal cultures in institutions had weakened; political parties were hollow shells; civil society was atomised and fragmented. At the same time, the sphere of the state and the regulatory had extended.

The sociologist Michael Moran describes this as 'the shift from the tacit to the explicit – from a world of broad informal understandings to one where arrangements become more precisely codified'. Everywhere there was 'the reconstruction of self-regulatory institutions along more formally organised, more codified, and more state controlled lines'.[37] This included the subjection of public institutions to independent regulators, and also the 'colonisation' of areas of civic life such as the 'the hitherto autonomous, self-referential worlds of individual sports' with the creation of policy bodies such as Sport England.

The state regulation that developed in the late 1990s and early 2000s did not represent a process of classic bureaucratisation or democratic rationalisation. The theories of state regulation that appeared at this time indicate that this was a quite different phenomenon. This was not the state as a bureaucratic hierarchy, but as mediator, supervisor and surveyor, a go-between: in the jargon of the time it was not a 'doer' but a 'steerer' of the actions of others. This new state was described variously as a 'managerial revolution', 'regulatory state', or an 'audit society'. These concepts represented the development of the state as flexible third-party authority, not a grand organiser but a moderator between parties. The new state is not a subject but an interrogator or supervisor of the actions of others.

Therefore, these new forms of state regulation emerged from the crisis of state institutions and social forms, of elite and working classes, as their respective social-interest formations unravelled. The officious state cannot be said to serve elite interests in the way of the old 'club' institutions or a classic bureaucracy. The new state is not a new social interest but the immanent response to the crisis of the old.

It is notable that the officious state is particularly an Anglo-Saxon form, and is much less developed in countries retaining a classic bureaucracy and some formations of social interest. For example, French society remains organised to a significant extent in blocks of social interest. Almost every week someone is marching on Paris or paralysing rail and road: teachers, students, Breton farmers in their tractors, transport unions, doctors. Although less politicised than before, these groups still exist as units which impose demands and negotiate terms with the government.

In France one hardly sees the new busybody official. Officials are of the old school: they are servants of a machine organised on classic bureaucratic lines. They are courteous but haughty; they bear the prestige of state function at their backs. State administration is still its own world, its own special and specific art, and the brightest of each generation still sign up at the École Nationale d'Administration to be moulded for the elite cadres of 'haut functionaires'. They still talk about 'serving the state'.[38] This state structure may exist in 'splendid and derisory isolation' from society, as one book on the state of French bureaucracy complained,[39] but nonetheless these procedures represent an abstraction of some social function, with trains running on time and rubbish collected, and at the lower level retains a public-service ethic and remains responsive to public need.

It is only where state institutions and social structures have unravelled to a complete degree that we see the new officious state forms rise up in their place.

This leaves England, which historically had the most independent civil society in Europe, with one of the most regulated. George Orwell wrote in 1941 that English communal life was defined by the fact that it was 'not official': 'All the culture that is most truly native centres round things which even when they are communal are not official – the pub, the football match, the back garden, the fireside and the "nice cup of tea"'. Orwell also noted the characteristic English dislike of interfering officials: 'The most hateful of all names in an English ear is Nosey Parker'.[40] (Indeed, there was very strong resistance to the formation of a police service in the early 19th century because people disliked the idea of being spied upon.) The British state is now far more implicated in the interstices of social life than the state in France, where there remains a popular mistrust of bureaucracy and a resourcefulness at avoiding or ignoring regulatory demands which appear too arduous.

Bureaucracy for itself

The ultimate cause of the officious state lies in the vacuum in civic life, since all state structures have their origin in civil society rather than in themselves. And yet the initiative comes from the state. There is a way in which the officious state has become a subject, a *bureaucracy-for-itself*. Officiousness is in essence a state-like ideology, an ideology which represents the interest of and vantage point of the state structure.

The officious state is *the subject-official*, in response to *the non-subject public*. This is the meaning of busybody meddling: it is the assertion of the official into the vacuum of public life.

Officiousness is the ideology of an emptied-out state structure, stripped both of links to society and its own distinct institutional cultures. These institutions were created by their own distinct histories and popular pressure, but when these social bases have gone what is left is the sheer institutional form, the bureaucratic infrastructure. These state institutions once had their own constituency and internal life; now what remains is the sheer *state structure occupied by officials*. This is defined primarily by its detachment from society, the fact that it is raised above social life and separated from it. The independence and oppositional nature of the capitalist state creates the precondition for it to develop as a truly independent and oppositional form.

The new bureaucracy fetishises the power of its own procedures, since these are all it knows and the only weapons it possesses. These officials are left only with the apolitical mechanisms and tools of bureaucracy: forms, databases, policies, surveillance.

Bureaucratic language and thought – the neutral, impersonal, of no particular position – is the language that remains after the collapse of politics and of political positions. When there are no camps to represent, one instead talks from the position of the no-camp, the blank abstract authority above camps. When the social has imploded, the point of authority that remains is outside the social, deliberately apart from it and set against it. Bureaucratic forms come into their own because they appear not to depend upon interest formations; they appear to be their own origin and referent.

Officious mechanisms perform some of the functions previously performed by social institutions, if in a partial and unsatisfactory manner. The database, the form, the policy or the search become the new forms of integration, the new forms of discipline and common rituals. There is a way in which the lifting of one's arms for the search, the application for a licence, or the submission of oneself for vetting provide a certain structure for social incorporation, as well as a new basis for institutional authority.

In place of individual participation in a social institution there is instead a structure of bureaucratic formalisation to which individuals are subjected. The mechanisms of bureaucracy start to become the basis of people's connection with the state, as well as forming the rituals of the age ('Everybody has submitted themselves') and some commonality and regimentation of conduct.

Institutional structure of the officious state

Starting in the 60s, Anthony Sampson's periodic *Anatomy of Britain* revealed the arcane, tight worlds behind closed doors of British institutions, each with its own language, personality type and internal culture.[41] Now we are seeing a blurring of institutional forms, as institutions start to take the same officious approach to their work and to their publics. Institutions that had been like different countries, different worlds, start to fuse into an indistinct body of *officialdom* and assume overlapping and cross-collaborational roles.

Police officers, council officials and private security guards assume overlapping remits and are frequently seen side by side. A private security guard will call the police for backup when somebody refuses to accept a fine; the police give powers to private security guards or council officials to confiscate alcohol or issue fines for criminal offences; council officers go on patrol with the police; councils empower private security guards to issue litter fines on their behalf. There is a similar institutional blurring in the USA: police officers go on patrol with officers from the Department of Corrections; the police can ban people from private property without asking the permission of the owner.[42]

Similarly, private businesses unite with the council to bring through bans on leafleting or public drinking, laws which are then enforced by the police – and all three sit on cross-institutional bodies such as 'safer-neighbourhood boards' and 'city-centre management' companies or 'safety-advisory groups'. This fusing of institutions has been deliberately driven by the government policy of 'partnership working'. In policy areas of child-protection or alcohol there is a blurring between the state sector, charities and private companies, who all offer 'child-protection training' in line with the 'latest procedures' or advice on 'responsible drinking practices'. People move easily between these different sectors. An organisation will start out as a charity, then become a company, while carrying out contracts for the state, and at the end of the day they all go to the same conferences and sit on the same 'child-safeguarding board'.

These different sectional interests would in the past have had very different roles: the police to prosecute crime and enforce public order, the council to deliver public services, private companies to defend their own business interests or those of their customers, charities to pursue a particular civic mission. These institutional forms developed in the 19th century and established the division of labour in the modern state.

The officious blurring of institutional forms is not a return to the pre-19th century state, however, which was based on skeleton and largely voluntary institutions, with different functions concentrated in the hands of gentry volunteers who exercised localised paternalistic control. What is occurring now is the fusing of different complex institutions into a blank, indistinct skin of state authority, which floats like an oil slick on the top of society. Institutions start to represent the vapid and instinct mission of officialdom-in-general.

Nor is this fusing the result of the dominance of the executive. In the Soviet Union the fusing of institutions was based on the predominance of the executive function, with a particular organ or individual eclipsing previously autonomous realms and competing forms of authority. The micromanagement of French society under the *ancien regime* was also the result of a pronounced executive, a central will which radiated out to every corner of the land through a network of agents (the *intendant* under the *ancien regime*, the prefect after the revolution).[43] Today's uniform category of officialdom is formed not by the dominance of the executive, but primarily by the decay of the old categories. The new official is what remains when the different institutional representatives have lost their particular colour and function, when they are no longer independent and self-referential worlds.

Increasingly the definition of a public official lies not in their public role or public status, but in their special status as set apart from ordinary people. This special coercive status (in the past restricted to the police) now becomes an attribute of transport workers, teachers and local authorities. Coercive powers have been handed out to public institutions of all kinds: hospitals gain powers to fine for offensive behaviour, teachers to fine for truancy or for parking outside schools, councils to fine for public order or minor misdemeanour.

The ordinary social authority figures in public places have waned – the park warden, the bus conductor, figures who had authority but no power. They performed a public function (collecting tickets, maintaining flowerbeds) but also kept order, telling off badly behaving children and breaking up fights. In their place come busybodies with power but no authority: people don't know who they are or where they are from, only that they bear power over them.

The reproduction of officiousness

The essential causative condition for officiousness is the vacuum in social life. It arises, as a negative form, from this situation of social vacuum. Yet the consequence of officious rules and regulations is to accentuate and reproduce this social vacuum, its essential condition. It is for this reason that officiousness reproduces itself as an automatic process, beyond the wills or interests of actors. Rules beget rules, procedures beget procedures.

For example, the waning of personal autonomy calls forth rules and procedures regulating personal comportment: the language one should use, the food one should eat. These rules then further undermine personal autonomy: the officious rule supplants the superego in the mind of the individual. This is turn creates further impetus for more rules and procedures.

Similarly, the crisis of civic life calls forth procedures and surveillance mechanisms to mediate people's relationships with one another. People begin to view each other with suspicion and mistrust, and so there are community wardens, anti-social behaviour hotlines, CCTV, the whole officious infrastructure which moves into and mediates these relationships. This infrastructure then further distances people from one another: the experience of relating through a third party means that they are less able to relate directly. After a while, they cannot do without it: there is no other way of relating.

Each round of officious procedures further evacuates social life, and reproduces the next round of procedures, even if it appears that nobody wills or wants this.

As the officious infrastructure mediates social relationships, it increasingly becomes the bearer of publicness and civility: this becomes what publicness *is*. In appealing to others, people need a sign to point to, so they can say, 'excuse me, this is a quiet coach', or 'this is a priority seat', or 'smoking is banned in this park'. It is not enough to appeal to the inconvenience caused to other members of the public or oneself; people talk to one other through codes, signs, rules. One assumes the position of enforcer of third-party authority, which is the singular source of civility and restraint.

Therefore, public life, inasmuch as it means anything, comes to mean codification and restraint. To be a good citizen means to obey official rules for comportment, no more and no less: to give up your seat when it is indicated you should do so, to use the correct language in order to avoid causing offence. There is no restraint on the basis of commonly held beliefs, or one's sensitivity to others, which were the traditional bases of civility. In public life there is only the raw individual, rampant and undirected, and then the inverse of this, the blank officious restraint. The choice is: officiousness or barbarism.[44]

Forced collaboration

The officious state has also spread through forced collaboration: co-opting members of the public into its ranks. It has become a condition of many kinds of civic activity that you appoint one of your member to play the role of the bureaucratic or behaviour-policing officer. The state effectively creates a network of agents, responsible for diffusing and enforcing officious policy.

Licensing law requires that every pub, village hall or community centre selling alcohol or holding 'regulated entertainment' appoint a named individual who is responsible for enforcing the licensing conditions. This person is the contact for the local authority: they submit applications, process paperwork and then enforce conditions (such as that they need to install CCTV or vet staff) and are responsible for any infractions.

Similarly, under the UK points-based visa system, any organisation inviting international speakers or visitors into the UK had to appoint a named individual to submit and process the required paperwork, such as fingerprints and bank statements. This person was then responsible for monitoring the visitor throughout their stay.

Even a small community group – an allotment group, or a village hall committee – is expected appoint a health-and-safety officer (responsible for public-liability insurance and risk assessments) and a child-protection officer (responsible for child-protection policies and criminal-records checks). If it is discovered that an organisation lacks such an individual, their activities could be suspended. Several organisations (including an allotment group and model-aircraft groups[45]) have closed down or excluded under-18s because they were unable to find anyone to act as child-protection officer.

This system of forced collaboration creates a mechanism for the diffusion of officious policy and procedure. It is because every local group has a child-safeguarding officer that the latest guidelines can diffuse into every church group and football club, in spite of their counter-intuitive and tortuous nature. These individuals are expected to keep up to date with the latest policy and go on training courses to learn about the group's responsibilities. Without such a network of agents officious documents would remain in official drawers and leave society untouched.

The compliance officer is loyal not to their group or to the sport, but to the state. The designated person is required to view the group with the eye of suspicion, to monitor their actions and to report any infractions, treating their neighbours or colleagues as foreign and unknown. They must ask a neighbour to complete a police check, even though they go around to their house for dinner and their children are friends. A person embedded in the community is required to step outside of that community, to take officious procedures and not their own experience as the basis for whether someone can or cannot be trusted.

There are hundreds of thousands of these appointed behaviour police: each church diocese, each football club, each community group. This becomes the new social structure, the new point of contact between the state and civil society; this replaces the party structures or civic organisations which stretched from Westminster down to each village or small town. These are the channels through which the state communicates;

these are its allies.

The difference, of course, is that safeguarding officers are not party members, but appointed officers. Many perform their role not of their own free will but often because they have no choice. So the structure which links state and society originates not primarily from below, in society, but from above, in the officious state. Given the opportunity many of these volunteers would hand in their badges and get back to the football field. They talk in weary tones, like martyrs ('*somebody* has to do it') as if their own sacrifice through tedium were the condition for everybody else being able to get on with things.

This structure also creates an opportunity for the genuinely officious people – the tut-tutters and curtain-twitchers, who in a previous age were ignored – to step forward into leadership roles. Many compliance officers are doing it because they have to, but others seize the opportunity and step forward into these new positions of social importance. It is often the case that in a small organisation the same individual is safeguarding officer, whistle-blowing officer and health-and-safety officer, as if they were made for this role. (There is a difference between formal status and genuine respect, however: it has been said, *sotto voce*, that the safeguarding officer is 'the person you would definitely not leave your children with'.)

Officious class interest

We have emphasised that the officious state is not like a classic self-interested clique, monopolising social resources for its own aggrandisement. However, officious officers and organisations do have a self-interest in the maintenance and spread of officiousness: the coordinators of training courses have an interest in the expansion of training requirements, compliance officers have an interest in the production of more guidance and procedures.

There are a number of 'officious industries', which represent a new kind of internal economy. Before you can organise a boys' football match you must pay for child-protection training, criminal-records checks, public-liability insurance. Before you can hand out leaflets you must buy a leafleting licence (£350 for a Saturday in Basildon and £262 per distributor in Wolverhampton)[46]; before you can busk in Camden you must apply for a busking licence (the fee is not returned if the application is rejected). This fee maintains the officious infrastructure: people's leafleting licenses cover the cost of bureaucrats to issue and administer the licence system; the criminal-background check fee maintains the apparatus of organisations that perform these checks. Some parent volunteers are asked to pay a portion of the police check fee before they can listen to reading in their children's school.[47]

This economy of fees and fines is a structured relationship between the public and the state, a systematic flow of social resources towards maintaining an officious infrastructure. These fees and fines become increasingly important in the economy of public authorities – for example, as a portion of local-authority income. Some sections of the state are independent bodies, financially independent of their master departments, and make their living entirely from fees such as checks or licences.[48]

There is also a parasitic industry which offers 'services' to mediate between the public and obstructive regulations. Organisations offer 'child-protection training' to 'educate' organisations about the steps they should be taking. Complicated visa systems encourage the growth of companies offering 'visa services' to help you to fill in your visa application form. Requirements for risk assessments create a market for insurance companies providing the paperwork for your street party or event. Contractors offer 'bullying-mediation services', 'energy-efficiency advice', 'smoking-cessation techniques' and so on.

These are essentially agents who mediate between a hostile

bureaucracy and the public, enabling compliance. It may appear that your agent is helping you, since you pay him, but your agent is actually helping the state, since the goal is to enable you to comply with its unworldly requirements.

Seen as a whole, officiousness has a particular structural-economic relationship to the rest of society. In this sense, it could be called a class. This class has an interest in the maintenance and expansion of the officious infrastructure, in the expansion of checks, monitoring and licensing, which in one way or another is paid for by the public.

Wealth is used neither for the personal consumption of the elite, nor for productive or public benefit, but instead starts to be used *for the reproduction and expansion of bureaucratic mechanisms*.

Thus the officious class is a parasitic class in the true sense of the word. It monopolises public resources for the maintenance of its own hostile body. People must pay for the privilege of being checked and monitored, a process which subordinates them to state authority and contributes to their obstruction and frustration.

The officious class has none of the redeeming features of self-aggrandising cliques, who nonetheless did something of import with the surplus they skimmed off (statues, vanity building projects). Even blowing money on extravagant parties or parades has something to be said for it: something of value was done.

Never before has a class monopolised social resources for such little productive effect, or rather, to such entirely negative effect.

4

Officious language

Officious vocabulary

Officious language is a strange breed, quite unlike everyday language.

The signature officious words are 'appropriate' and 'inappropriate', words that are quite devoid of moral judgement or other values. An act is evaluated not by its worldly results (its intentions or effects, whether it helped or hurt people) but in terms of whether it measured up with a code of conduct or protocol. To say something is 'inappropriate' is a question of non-compliance with official standards of behaviour or comportment. 'Inappropriate' involves a sniffy observation that a box has not been ticked (which is quite distinct from a departure from social or moral norms, since these imply the pressure of a disapproving community that is shocked or moved by the deviant conduct).

A wide variety of incidents are transcribed into these blank indifferent terms. 'Inappropriate' could refer to something entirely trivial such as a slightly risqué comment, or something very grave and serious such as a child's death after social-service failures.

'Appropriate' and 'inappropriate' are therefore false norms, rooted not in social life but grounded in bureaucratic life and the officious realm. The problem is not that they are produced by an elite, but that they are quite devoid of human sentiment or the experience of any social class.

Cousin officious words are 'best practice' and 'poor practice'; there is also 'recommended practice' or 'advised practice'. It is significant that 'practice' is the officious word for actions, since this suggests not a consciously chosen act, with inner meaning and intention, but standardised modes of conduct existing in predefined forms which one reproduces. Actions are also described as 'behaviour' – as in, 'inappropriate behaviour' or 'expected behaviour' – which has that same estranged quality of judging an action only by its external manifestations.

Some ordinary words have been taken up into officious language and assumed a quite different meaning. One of these is 'responsible', a word that in ordinary language means one's obligation to others, an institution or office, but in officious language means one's ties to officialdom or to a set of codes. Under licensing laws a group or institution must appoint a 'responsible person' who takes charge of implementing various licensing requirements. One's 'responsibilities' means a list of things one must do: a 'responsible person' is therefore also known as a 'compliance officer'.

'Safe' and 'unsafe' have gone through a similar transformation, now meaning compliance with codes of best practice: to comply is 'safe', to not have done so is 'unsafe'. 'Safe drinking', 'safe events', 'safe photography' – all these really mean 'regulated', i.e. an event where one has done risk assessments, drawn up codes of conduct, given people badges and official roles.

When one's practice has fallen short of 'best practice' it is described as 'disappointing': 'this is very disappointing behaviour'; 'the failure to abide by the policy is disappointing'. Again, what is at issue is one's divergence from (which is cast as a falling short of) a procedural code or protocol. 'Disappointing' means only a sniffy note of disapproval at an incident of non-compliance. It can also be applied to a range of actions – anything from an injudicious word to drunken riots – since these very different events are transposed onto an essentially procedural plane.

Officious language also invents new terms which have no ordinary meaning, such as the shift from 'child protection' to 'child safeguarding'. 'Safeguarding', a term that was rarely used in normal speech, has become the primary term for social work and children's services, and can be used in a variety of constructions: 'this school is safeguarding children', 'these are safeguarding responsibilities', or 'child-safeguarding is very important to us'. Its present-continuous form suggests a constant bearing.

'Safeguarding' is not in fact about one's relationships to children, but about one's relationships to authority, to the official codes specifying how one should relate to children. Thus one does not say 'I look after children' but 'I take my safeguarding responsibilities seriously'. This statement means that one is attempting to comply with the standards such as always having adults work in twos, leaving doors open, carrying out criminal-records checks and drawing up requisite procedures and codes.

Finally, officious language has a topsy-turvy 'double-speak' quality. One example of this is 'community-support officer' to describe an officer who fines people and tells them to stop doing things. Zones within which people must buy a licence to leaflet are described as 'consent to the distribution of free-literature zones'; a no-alcohol zone is called a 'designated public-place order'; an area where activities are banned is called a 'public-spaces protection order'. Unfreedom is presented as freedom. Vetting and other procedures are not imposed but are 'available': you are 'eligible' for criminal-records checks, you are 'included' in a monitoring scheme, and a public space is surveyed 'for your protection'. Officiousness is presented not as an imposition but as the definition of publicness and public space, into which people are generously included and helped to do the right thing.

One NSPCC child-protection document shows many of these common officious words in use: '*Safe Sport Events, Activities and Competitions* will help you to ensure that you meet the safeguarding responsibilities for your event...'

Language and the eclipse of meaning

Officious phrases seem to exist ready-made and can be picked up and bolted together as an occasion demands. It is demonstrative, a way of showing that one is au fait with what is expected but without saying anything in particular.

Officious language becomes the default form of public address. Somebody opening a public meeting will often start with an announcement about the fire exits and the restrictions on coffee cups or photography. Their words perform the role of a welcome but it is not a welcome. The words seem to flow through them and not be produced by them. As a result, the audience switches off: they expect the announcement, feel settled into the room and the event, accept that the person saying these words is in charge, but it is difficult to focus on what they are saying.

In this form it is relatively anodyne, perhaps, but officious language is also used in argument to assert superiority over others, to deliberately block a response.

When somebody says, 'this is unsafe practice which fails to meet with recommended procedures', it is not their opinion or an argument, but the impersonal and asocial injunction. People are told 'you have issues and need training' or 'your article was highly inappropriate and you would be advised to withdraw it', which is much more disarming than any profane criticism that invites opposing arguments in response.

Such language can be seen in almost every forum of public debate, from parliaments to online discussion groups. One local councillor complained of another: 'Cllr Edmunds has failed to abide by the equality policy she signed up to... by actively promoting discriminatory behaviour and I have written to the council making a formal complaint about her conduct. I also find it very disappointing that... the new Leader of the district council... has yet to speak out on this issue.'[49]

Here we see the bolting together of various elements: that

someone has 'failed to abide' by a 'policy' she 'signed up to', the 'formal complaint' about 'conduct', the 'disappointing' lack of response from others. While normal speech occurs in infinitely varied combinations, officious language is composed of a series of pre-fabricated elements which are reassembled. If the accusing councillor had continued, she would have called for the comments to be 'withdrawn' or for a 'formal apology'.

There is little that the offending councillor can say in response. Officious language is like a wall: you cannot argue or have a conversation with it. It is not a form of communication, but a form of white noise, which evacuates thought and blocks a response. The position it takes is outside social value or argument: it asserts its superiority over social meaning. Language is used as a stun-gun; the aim is for you to be silenced and to submit.

Officious language is the assumption of superiority founded on the neutralisation of opposing points of view (which are 'disappointing' and have 'failed to comply' with procedures).

The demand for an 'apology' is a call for the capitulation of the other person, for them to disavow their point of view, the reasons why they said or did what they did. The difference between a 'full apology' and a 'lukewarm apology' is that in the former the individual capitulates completely, whereas in the latter they stand a little by what they did or said. The half-apology would say 'I regret', whereas the full apology involves the stock-phrases: 'I would like to apologise for any hurt/offence caused by my words/actions. I did not intend to cause any hurt/offence and deeply regret any hurt/offence caused'. Words otherwise indicating profundity of feeling – 'deeply', 'unreserved', 'full', 'completely', 'sincerely' – function here as flags to indicate the degree of prostration.

In a debate it is common for both parties to try to play the officious part; these phrases are a means by which you manoeuvre yourself into the superior position and incapacitate your opponent. In doing this, these parties are committing a grave violation. They are bypassing the contest of views and argument, of rights and wrongs, by assuming the position of impartial, bureaucratic authority, which is not a party but a third party, detached from and set against society. The contest becomes not a contest of opposing views or interests but a contest to assume the position of bureaucratic authority.

Summary: officious language

Officious language is grounded in the procedural world; it is a coded reference to a superior form of authority, above the fray of everyday language and argument. The meaning of a word is not precise or concrete, but allusive. Therefore officious language is slightly different to managerial language, which is also technical and dry. Managerial language is used for exchanges between people on the same managerial level, referencing a world of managerial interchanges (techniques, status and so on) and so retains some precision.

Officious language is language that is used *against* others. It is like a plain-clothes policeman walking into a room and flashing a badge; the badge instantly places him above the other people in the room. To use officious language is to flash a badge. The word is not a bearer of precise understanding or content; it is an indicator of higher third-party status which is waved in the air. The listener doesn't hear any particular meaning; they feel words being used against them, over them.

Officious language is founded in the bureaucratic opposition to social life. It is not just that the words are devoid of meaning but that they are turned against the meaning of social life, against concrete passions and reasons, as a means to neutralise them and declare them null and void.

5

Red tape

Policy/code

A traditional policy would have meant a formalisation of commonly held beliefs about the way things should be done. The officious 'policy' is quite different: reading officious procedural documents is like entering a strange artificial world, using unfamiliar language and logic.

There are policies for areas of life that one would not have thought required any special rules: a 'lunchbox policy' specifying the contents of children's lunchboxes, a 'travel policy' specifying the recommended ways in which people might travel to work, a 'toileting policy' covering nappy-changing in a nursery. While schools might have a 'touch policy' or 'photography policy', departments of health have policies on how much alcohol one should drink or the number of fruits and vegetables one should eat each day. Organisations have a whistleblowing policy, privacy policy, diversity policy, equal-opportunities policy.

The content of these policies is relatively arbitrary. A touch policy may say that teachers can only touch a child 'lightly' or 'above the shoulder';[50] a school photography policy might state that parents can only take photos at a particular part of the play or only of their own child.[51] These are not intuitive distinctions. The virtue of a policy is merely that conduct has been regimented and laid down in a formal manner, and not left to people's judgement or spontaneous action.

It is as if these printed-out pieces of paper (though invariably copied off the internet) hold within themselves the capacity to ward off harm. It would be unthinkable that, for example, a volunteering organisation could carry out an activity without a child-protection policy, health-and-safety policy or equal-opportunities policy. Nothing counts that is not written down: only the paper world matters. If one has no policy on children's welfare then apparently one does not care about children. If you have no privacy policy then apparently you will sell your subscribers' email addresses to advertising companies.

There is a 12-step policy for dealing with bullying, a five-step whistleblowing procedure. The aim is for the stages of conduct to be laid out, step by step, so that nothing is left open to choice or chance. In the case of a dispute: person A fills in a form and sends it to the designated bullying/whistleblowing officer, who will respond within x days and arrange a meeting, after which a report will be prepared... Each event is classified as bullying/whistleblowing/discrimination, and then dealt with using the relevant formula.

Policies also include ethical statements, with sports groups saying that 'children's welfare is very important to us' or 'every child has a right to enjoy sporting activity'. Once ethics is transmuted into this odd and formal statement the activity is emptied of intrinsic ethical content, and becomes forced and artificial. Ethics only exists as sanctioned by an external authority; as if, were it not for the policy, coaches would not want children to enjoy sport.

While a traditional policy should be intuitive, the formalisation of right thinking, an officious policy is defined by its non-intuitive character and its perversion of right thinking and right reason. In its essence it is stilted and strange, and the strangeness of a policy becomes part of its commendation.

That is, it is defined not just by the fact that it is not-free, regimented, but also in that it is not-normal, that it is artificial and a negation of normal behaviour and involves an estrangement from normal instincts and obligations. Golf clubs have 'late-collection guidelines' (what to do in the event of a child's parents not coming to pick them up) which prohibit the one thing that would be the logical and humane thing to do: take the child home. The list of 'actions' may include calling the police, but never the obvious thing that would solve the child's need to go home.[52]

One's obligations to others are supplanted by an obligation to the officious code, and one is supposed to sacrifice a person before one deviates from a policy or code. Even extremely unethical action can be justified by the defence that you were 'following recommended guidelines'. Once, two police community-support officers stood and watched a child drown, saying that they should not intervene without the requisite training.[53] The child's mother said she 'can't understand it. You don't have to be trained to jump in after a drowning child. If you're walking down the street and you see a child drowning you automatically go in that water.'

People relate to others through procedural mechanisms, and are held to account and are judged by the code and not by the consequences of their actions upon other people. The result is behaviour that we 'cannot understand', since it is based on a repression of what an ordinary person would 'automatically' do in that situation.

The final significant feature of officious policies is that they change all the time: there is always a new round of 'updated guidance' or 'latest best practice'. This is not incidental; policies are supposed to change, and one of the obligations upon an organisation is that they periodically review and update their policies. Many policies come with an expiry date of a year.

The meaning of this churn of policy is that it is everyone's responsibility to keep up to date with the latest guidance and officious trend. This means a constant openness of oneself to officious authority. You cannot just learn a policy and get on with it, but instead should be receptive and alert for the latest instructions. The churn of policy keeps everybody attuned and ready to switch behavioural patterns, and undermines any opportunity for developing autonomy or settling on any particular lines of action.

Licence

Licences are a defining legal form in pre-modern or totalitarian societies. Until the late 1600s every printed product had to bear the licenser's stamp, without which it was a criminal item. The tendency in the democratic-constitutional state was to free social life from requiring permission slips. In modern times licences were limited to dangerous or controlled activities (owning wild animals or guns) or markets subject to special controls or taxes, such as street trading licences.[54]

With the rise of officiousness there has been a resurgence of the licence form, which has spread to include the political-public sphere as well as the most everyday of activities. This means a transformation of the civic and public sphere, such that action is mediated through the gaining of formal permission.

There are licences covering key aspects of public-political life: holding a political demonstration, setting up a campaign stall in a city street, or holding a charity collection.

At the more informal level, in different parts of the UK there are licences for: dancing, busking,[55] handing out leaflets,[56] fitness instructors in parks,[57] taking wedding photos in parks.[58] Under the UK 2003 Licensing Act's 'regulated entertainment' provision, even a solitary guitar player in a pub needed a 'provision of regulated entertainment licence', and the mere possession of a piano in an old people's home required a 'provision of entertainment facilities licence'. New York clubs must obtain a dancing licence before their punters can legally sway to music, and the police have carried out raids on sites of unlicensed dancing.

Thus do pleasure and entertainment become state-sanctioned and authorised activities. One Cambridge pub was told they needed a 'spoken-word licence' for a poetry performance. Even that most ancient form of entertainment requires authorisation; you need a piece of paper before opening your mouth. The landlord protested that they already had a music licence for concerts but the council official insisted that it was a matter of principle: 'Licences are there to be adhered to... there need to be checks in place... When somewhere does not have a spoken-word licence they are not permitted to hold events such as plays and poetry readings, regardless of the other performances they are able to hold.'[59]

The actual content of these licences is not that important. It is not the case that licences come with strict forms of political or social control, as they did in Maoist China, where the requirement for a travel or marriage licence was the means by which the authorities moved people around the country like chess pieces. Officious licences often come with relatively few conditions and are given out with little distinction.

The form of restraint and restriction lies in the licence form itself, in the requirement that one can only publish, protest or dance with official authorisation. One must go through the officious procedure before acting; one must have applied and gained the stamp of authorisation. To neglect to ask permission is itself a criminal offence, the offence of unlicensed activity.

This is the key meaning of the licence, and its key problem. In John Milton's protest against print licensing in 1644, *Areopagitica*, he said: by all means prosecute seditious books, but do not criminalise a book on the sole basis that it is unauthorised; do not criminalise the sheer fact that it is freely published without first passing under the licenser's stamp.

Over 300 years after the end of print licensing, the systems that were dismantled at the birth of modern society are being built back up in a new guise. The instinct that all activities must be licensed has spread throughout public authority, to the extent that we see a reversal of the basis of the liberal state: from the assumption that everything is allowed unless it is specifically prohibited, to the assumption that everything is banned unless it is specifically allowed.

Often people will be asked to produce licences that don't actually exist: a 'photography licence' for taking photos in public, for example, or a 'megaphone licence'[60] for political protesters. Others may be asked for a letter of authorisation from some or other authority. The assumption is that some form of paperwork must be present to justify whatever they are doing, an assumption which overreaches the actually existent forms of paperwork.

Many people have internalised this assumption and line up to do the necessaries and obtain requisite permission. On occasion they have even invented their own licences. Some children's sports groups make parents 'register' their camera by writing their names in a book, or they produce 'licensed photographer' armbands for parents for which they must apply each year.[61] In these cases, the group authorises themselves, performing for themselves the role of the officious licensing authority, being their own third party and stamping their own form.

Someone taking professional photos in public, especially of children, often carries around printouts of their contract or wears their press card or a day-glo jacket. This phenomenon of *self-authorisation* demonstrates that officiousness also has roots in civil society, in people's sense of the illegitimacy of their own free action.

While free activity is held to be inherently criminal and dangerous, licensed action is seen as inherently safe and civilised. This is a sheer act of faith: there is nothing to stop a paedophile or terrorist from obtaining a photography licence if they so desire. The licence form is seen as a civilising power which is supposed to endow restraint at a stroke.

At base, the belief is that the problem is always freedom and the answer is always restraint, bureaucracy which through its sheer obstructiveness is supposed to civilise those who pass through its torrid channels.

Contracts

Unlike the licence, the contract is a capitalist legal form par excellence: individuals with conflicting interests negotiating a deal by which both are bound. A contract embodies the wills of the parties, but it also empowers the presiding third party with legal authority, as a witness and enforcer of the contract.

The contract form used to mainly exist in areas of life where people faced each other as conflicting and opposed, such as economic exchange or labour relations. Now it has expanded into new areas of life, from schools to public institutions, and has become applied to much more complex domains of activity. In this new form, the contract is one of the primary means for the extension of officious authority. Complex social relationships are formalised and conducted as if there were a lawyer or official in the room; people are held to account not by each other, nor by their common enterprise, but by the paperwork both have signed.

Universities make contracts with their students, and schools with their pupils, laying out the behavioural elements expected of both parties and the sanctions for behavioural breaches. A conference convenor may make a 'contract' with the attendees, pledging that they will deliver the programme containing specified elements to a requisite standard, in exchange for specified behaviour from the attendees.

The officious contract recasts these common social enterprises into narrow relations of conflict, subject to the same legal strictures as that of economic exchange. Yet while the economic contract or legal dispute is a genuine expression of a relationship – it arises from the reality of the relationship of conflicting interests – these new contracts are an artificial imposition on a relationship, supplanting more meaningful ways of relating or discussing.

The contract formalises people's understanding of what they seek to achieve and what they owe each other. In turn, the contract tends to transform the relationship into one between people with hostile opposed interests who are held to account not by their mutual obligation or substantial goals, but by the third party of officious authority. They are held to account by the form they have signed. Thus an informal relationship that was self-mediated becomes mediated through a third party, which stands above their two wills and balances the profit and loss of each.

A common enterprise such as educating students becomes a matter of the compelled delivery of services by each party. Teachers, students and parents have a list of 10 or so things to which they agree: 'The pupil will be correctly dressed and equipped for school; the school will ensure that all pupils are valued and encouraged to achieve their full potential; parents will attend parents' evenings and discussions about my child's progress'. The pedagogical relationship is consequently narrowed; the question becomes whether the parties have met their side of the deal.

Officious paperwork defines and structures an encounter, and becomes that which each takes away from it. Some PhD students write reports about the 'outcomes' from every meeting with their tutor, which then they both sign. The student takes away not new ideas but the signed piece of paper.

Here we see how the bad faith at the base of officiousness – the assumption that people are out to get one another – empowers the third party of officious authority to preside over these conflictual relations. The simplest exchange needs to be specified and laid down in advance, to keep both parties in check. Paperwork becomes the check upon and regulator of relations.

The contract has even moved into the inner life of the individual, with 'commitment contracts' made through websites such as StickK. Here a person's goal to stop smoking or to exercise are formalised and mediated through a third party, with defined goals, appointed judges, and penalties for non-compliance. Thus the contract form – the formal agreement through an outside party – replaces one's inner dialogue with oneself and the exertion of willpower.

Finally, we see the expanded use of the contract by institutions to replace more traditional forms of authority. Rather than give a badly behaved child a telling off, or to attempt to help them, a school or local authority will increasingly ask them to sign an 'acceptable-behaviour contract'. This will specify the required behaviour ('I will go to school/I will not climb on rooftops or throw things at people'), the period for which the behaviour is agreed, and the penalties for breaking the contract.

Therefore we see that bureaucratic-legal authority replaces other forms of authority for the child. Badly behaving children find themselves faced not with disciplining or angry people, whose disciplining is driven by care for that child, but with a dispassionate *legal infrastructure*, specifying the precise 'behaviour' they are expected to manifest if they are to avoid given sanctions. Legalistic paperwork replaces the moral education of a child and their integration into areas of common social enterprise.

Consent forms

A related officious mechanism is the *consent form*, which has also moved into informal spheres of life. People sign forms to 'consent' to have their photograph taken, to have their child's photograph taken, or to have their child's photograph published in a school book or sent to a pen friend. A formidable infrastructure has developed around sexual activity in certain American colleges, drawing up consent forms so the parties can agree to the different stages of seduction, or else requiring that each stage of sexual activity is agreed explicitly in words ('Any form of sexual activity to which both people did not verbally consent is not allowed')[62] or that a couple photograph themselves together with a 'consent kit'.[63] US states including New York and California have legislated on the question of 'affirmative-consent standards' in high schools and universities.

The form replaces consent given in the course of an action or relationship, the tacit reading of gestures and signs, whereby the subject communicates to the photographer that they don't mind being photographed or two people agree to go to bed. Instead the deal is stated beforehand, so the activity is not a discovery of boundaries but the playing out of pre-agreed terms. It is not a simple and direct relation between two people, but one mediated through an independent authority.

The question of consent is a question of what has been made clear to this other authority, which will specify what 'counts as' consent ('saying it in words', taking a photo, or filling in a form: in every case something extraneous to the activity and the moment). People are subject to controls and judgements that are not inherent in the relation, but imposed and external to it.

The relationship between photographer and subject, or between lovers, is re-presented as a taking of one by the other, a violation and breaching of the boundaries of the self to which one must formally consent. As if our natural state is not to touch, not to relate, and that we consent to being touched only very deliberately. Here we see how officious authority is extended through the contamination of the human relationship and the transmuting of people into two opposed parties.

The consent form becomes our defence against each other, for the 'taken' to specify limits, and for the 'taker' to prove that the other agreed and cannot sue afterwards. The bureaucratic-legal form becomes the guarantor and moderator, specifying the boundaries and duration of the action. Increasingly it becomes the precursor to a social relation: before people come into relation, paperwork must be completed and signed. *So it appears, in some way, that it is paperwork that brings us into relation with one another.*

Risk assessments

Before one holds a concert, takes children to the museum, or introduces a new policy, one must complete a formal assessment of the risks entailed in the activity.

Ordinary parts of the physical or social world are analysed in the terms of a hazard, given labels such as 'moving vehicles', 'trip hazards', 'noise', 'electrical appliances' and 'crowd intensity'. A concert becomes the site of noise, electrical appliances and crowd intensity: a social activity is re-presented from the estranged position of an observer who views it as a hazard with bio-physical reverberations.

The risk assessment embodies the officious view of free activity: that it is a dubious disturbance of the world which is likely to have negative and unforeseen effects. In the officious mind, any action is seen primarily not in terms of what could be gained, but in terms of the possibility of negative consequences.

Reading risk-assessment guidelines, one has the feeling that the author has never seen or done the thing they are talking about. A headmaster might risk assess the activity of cartwheels (as if he had never heard of such an unnatural thing, children spinning upside down) and allot it a risk of 3 out of 5, which means it must be carried out with supervision. One cathedral carried out risk assessments of its flower arrangers, concluding that thorns and prickles were found on flowers and therefore the flower arrangers should wear gloves.[64]

As with other officious mechanisms, the role of the risk assessment is to require that you fill in a form before you act: you cannot go on a school trip, hold a street party or concert without the piece of paper in your pocket. More than this, the risk assessment is also an ideological warning against the dangers of independent action. Once you have filled in a risk-assessment form you may conclude that your activity is not worth the bother after all.

When every action is seen from the aspect of a potential hazard, the tendency is always to close down, cancel, shutdown. In the language of risk assessment, once one has identified a 'hazard', one must 'consider removal of this hazard' or 'consider preventing access to this hazard'. The inevitable result of a risk assessment is the suppression and obstruction of people's activity; once they have been so 'assessed' it is very likely that the pancake race or conkers contest will not go ahead.

This legal form, more than any other, embodies the wrinkled nose of suspicion and doubt at the wisdom of most things that most people are doing. It seeks most purposefully to obstruct and limit, and tends most consistently towards restriction and the officious ideal of inaction.

Risk assessments are also used pragmatically as a way of stopping activities of which authorities disapprove: they go in with clipboards and dubious expressions. One is 'risk assessed', put through a clinical procedure, and then it is 'recommended' that whatever you are doing is 'unsafe' or requires 'further procedures to be put in place'.[65] Several councils require that political protesters provide risk assessments of their stalls (Swindon Council requires that a risk assessment be filled in every month, while Woking Council also requires public-liability insurance and a photo of the stall and any literature).[66]

A related phenomenon is the growth of public-liability insurance, which increasingly must be obtained for almost any public activity: holding a street party or meeting, handing out leaflets, or even putting up a poster on a lamppost.[67] Here your action into the public world is recast as a liability, as a potential for you to harm other people and for other people to sue you. Public-liability insurance is like a caution tax, a payoff and an absolution for acting in the world. This represents the death of civic action and public spirit: it means that any initiative into the public realm requires a lawyer at your side, to protect the public from you and you from the public.

It is important to emphasise that these procedures are not a greater insurance against accident. In fact, they encourage one to hold more store by the paper trail than by one's own judgement, which can mean a weakened ability to assess the consequences of one's activity. The primary aim of a risk assessment is not really to prevent accident, but to leave a paper trail such that if an accident happens it is not your fault. It is like a talisman, if not exactly warding off misfortune then insulating you from its repercussions.

Training

There has been a great explosion of training courses and qualifications (diversity-awareness training, health-and-safety courses, child-protection courses, smoking-cessation courses, e-safety training) and a related community of trainers and experts.

Before you take on a position of authority (whether a dentist or a horse-riding instructor) you must generally have been on a course or several courses, with certificates to show that you have been trained in 'diversity issues', child-protection procedures or health and safety.

Training is not there to impart useful skills (as first-aid training taught resuscitation techniques or how to give injections) but is instead a process of education in officious forms of behaviour. The course promises to 'enhance awareness and good practice' and impart 'the latest legislation and guidance'. The role of training is a kind of 'qualification in officiousness': to be a scout or a dance teacher one must equally have been educated in officious thought and behaviour.

There are three levels of child-protection courses, each requiring more hours to endure, and each designed for people of increasing responsibility within an organisation or with a closer relationship with children. As you move up the course levels, the distinguishing feature of the level-3 training course is the amount of official policy with which one must become familiar. The certificate is generally valid for two or three years, after which time the course must be repeated. The refresher course updates attendees on the 'latest guidance': in this way, people are periodically brought into contact with the latest officious thinking.

If one moves into management the possibilities for being trained increase further, with courses on working with others, minute-taking, getting the most from your meetings, strategic thinking, managing performance positively, developing yourself as manager, transformational leadership training, agile leadership training. For management, training becomes a form of career progression and a socialisation into management ways of thinking. It becomes the way in which the ambitious person develops themselves and moves up the ranks, gathering certificates as they go.

Trainers often perform the role of informal auditors when they visit institutions. A child-protection trainer will tell a photography gallery that there 'could be problems' with their programmes which involve children taking pictures of each other.[68] A university will be told that they lack 'proper procedures' for reporting cases of discrimination. An e-safety trainer may suggest that a school restrict parent photography at school events.[69]

The most significant role of training is to undermine ordinary forms of competence. It presents ordinary actions as special, as only permitted for people with a certificate or qualifications, which are delivered from without. The icon for a training course is a smiling trainer pointing out something on a flowchart, while attendees look up in rapt attention and take notes.

Ordinary human emotions and capacities are recast as special skills. Helping children is not seen as an ordinary part of adult life but a special activity carried out by qualified, designated people. You are only sensitive to children, apparently, if you have achieved the mantel of 'designated safeguarding officer': only such a person would have the 'skills' to recognise that bruises or a child being withdrawn could be 'signs of abuse'. This turns emotions and ordinary capacities into something artificial and specialised, rather than an element of common sense based on one's sensitivity to others.

The role of the course is to undermine free action, *to sell social life back to itself but as something external and not its own* – and then to give a certificate which is a permission slip, to say you have been trained and therefore are allowed. Similarly, things that are learnt in the course of a vocation such as leadership or strategy are packaged into nuggets and sold back to people: 'by the end of this course you will appreciate how to turn strategy into operational plans'. Training is the alienation from one's own capacities, the projection of these capacities onto an outside source which then delivers them unto you as part of a formula.

As a result, the more courses you have been on the less you are able to do. The process of training is really a training out of ordinary ways of thinking, a desensitisation to ordinary ways of thinking and talking (an education out of these) and a certain dehumanisation whereby instinctive responses are suppressed and you evaluate the world from official points of view.

A child-protection course will leave you less able to work with children or to help them. You will be told that it's 'better to avoid' the situation of giving a child a lift home, that it is better to avoid touching them in the course of a music or dance lesson, that you should seek to avoid forming relationships with children. So the trained person is left incapacitated, arms pinned to their sides, unable to deal with a child who can't get home or to guide a violin bow into the correct position. The more certificates they have, the less somebody can meet the needs of their profession or those around them.

Audit

The practice of auditing was subject to an early and prescient critique by Michael Power, who identified that the issue was not assessment or inspection per se, but the *ideology of the audit*: a question of the *external* and *quantifiable* verification of professional activity. He described the 'audit explosion' as 'checking gone wild': 'ritualised practices of verification whose technical efficacy is less significant than their role in the production of organisational legitimacy'.[70] Today this audit explosion has continued and spread into new areas, with energy-efficiency audits, safeguarding audits, diversity audits, sexuality and homophobia audits.

Power argued that the audit is based on a faith placed in the 'authority of distance' (the outside observer) and in 'formality' as an end in itself. He noted how audits transformed institutions, which were 'colonised' by the constant experience of outside assessment, such that 'research was organised in order to be assessable'[71] and professionals had an 'anxious preoccupation with how one is seen by others'.[72] Alternatively, the institution split into two, with a special organ for dealing with external audits in order to 'buffer' and protect the mainstay of professional work. This creation of a separate organ indicates the essential conflict of interest between the demands of audit and the life of the institution.

The audit was an early embodiment of the figure of third-party authority and of officious regulation. The essential elements observed by Power in the 1990s can now be seen in different forms of new regulation, as described in this chapter, each of which represents a particular form of legality and subjectivity. Taken together, this body of regulation is quite distinct from both modern and pre-modern regulation.

Officious regulation in context

The different forms of modern regulation are derived from the free will of individuals or groups. The contract or civil legal form is derived from the conflicting wills of individuals. The Marxist legal theorist Evgeny Pashukanis argued that all Western law could be derived from the 'cell form' of the simple dispute, from the 'two litigating parting who, vindicta in hand, claim their right'.[73] He counterposed this to technical regulation such as a railway timetable or traffic plan, which is derived from the needs of a group of people where relations do not conflict: it is the simple, neutral rule, which organises relations efficiently among a group of people. Therefore, modern regulation differs in form according to the nature of the free relations embodied in it, and whether these are conflicting or non-conflicting.

Pre-modern regulation, by contrast, governs a social life in which the subjective principle has not yet emerged. Regulation does not express the free will of individuals or groups, but instead determines conduct and relations from without: it stamps itself upon social life. For example, in ancient China, says Hegel, 'all is directed and superintended from above'; 'Everything is arranged with the greatest minuteness'.[74] The questions of disposition or relations within a family are settled by given rules. A son must not leave a room without his father's permission; parents' graves must be visited annually; the husband must love his first wife more than the others. Right conduct was a question of following the rule which was supplied from without; ethical life was governed by threats of external sanctions. Regulation provides the content for social life: the law forms collective life and determines the conduct of individuals towards one another.

Officious regulation is quite different. It does not embody the free will of the parties, but nor does it determine social life or stamp itself upon it. It has instead a particular negative relation to free subjectivity. It exists as the moderator, auditor, regulator of free subjectivity: its role is not to impose a new social content but only to mean that an action cannot be carried out freely and on its own terms.

Therefore, you can hand out leaflets but you must buy a licence first; you can organise an event but you must carry out a risk assessment; you can have sex but you must fill in a consent form. The regulation is not determining the content of an action but instead is supervising and formalising a relation that is otherwise determined by the parties. The officious regulation is a formality which acts as a check or impediment upon an action which is nominally free.

Unlike previous forms of regulation, officious regulation does not express the truth of the relations to which it is applied. Both the ancient Chinese code and modern contract law were true to the society and the particular relations that they governed. The regulation fitted the relation. Officious regulation lacks the essential rationality of previous regulatory forms. The formality of an officious policy or consent form violates the true content of a relation, making it artificial and stilted, but without giving it a new content. The consent form violates the true nature of the modern sexual relation, but not by imposing a new sexual morality or set of rules which give that relation a new meaning. The regulation violates the proper basis of a relation without giving it a new meaning.

It is therefore not a legal or regulatory form proper, but cod regulation, made-up regulation, which sounds and looks like regulation (there are subheadings and things to sign) but is not. The content is essentially arbitrary, it could take one form or another and changes constantly as one rule or code is replaced by another.

This is because officious regulation is produced only as the negation of free activity. Regulation does not restrict actions in the name of some alternative principle or truth. It has no content other than the antithesis of freedom, the pursuit of restraint and formality as an end in itself.

6

Surveillance

Cameras – the state

Security cameras would once have been restricted to private property, facing outward to guard against incursions along with the wire and the guard dogs. If there were cameras it meant you were not supposed to be there.

Now cameras define public spaces; they are facing across squares, on buses, in public buildings and restaurants. When a new public square is built the cameras are put in along with the benches and streetlights. Now if there are no cameras, you are not supposed to be there; if there are no cameras you must be in a no-man's land or wasteland, an unsafe and shadowy space. Public space has come to mean surveyed space.

Unwatched spaces are seen as disorderly and a threat to public order; if there is no camera then anything could happen. Hence the moves to put cameras in private minicabs, blank spots on the radar which are imagined to be a shady den of assault, robbery and vomiting women. Once people enter a cab they go off the radar and will go wild.

The role of the camera is to be the anonymous eye of officialdom who presides over and is present at every social situation. The role of the camera is to say, 'be careful, you are being watched', and it is this awareness of being watched that apparently endows people with restraint and consideration. It is the presence of cameras which makes a space public, indicates that it can be safely and legitimately used. If people are being watched they will be careful and not go wild.

The camera plays a symbolic rather than practical role, so it doesn't matter that many of the cameras are not working and most are just feeding a digital recorder: still they are endowed with a capacity to prevent crime and disorder. Members of the public often agree and say cameras make them feel safer. Fake CCTV cameras do this symbolic job just as well.

As we would expect from officiousness – the purely empty and negative authority – the camera is an absent-presence. Cameras watch silently, they do not act. The channelling of crime-prevention money into CCTV schemes in the 1990s marked the shift from the active police authority of the patrolling bobby to the omnipotent, lock-fast, impersonal eye of the camera. Indeed, watching has become an end in itself, a public service. It is announced with fanfare: yellow signs beaming 'Smile! You're on CCTV'; announcements on a loop that 'for your safety and security management, this area is monitored by 24-hour CCTV'. State surveillance was once carried out secretly; now it is a public performance, it rings in your ears and dazzles your eyes.

Cameras are a form of intervention into social life, but they are also a sign of the state's withdrawal from other ways of relating to the population. The camera becomes a replacement both for public order and public services, that is, for both discipline and provision.

When the police are faced with a public-order situation they often respond by getting their cameras out. Rioters are smashing things up and the police stand there filming them. After the riots in English cities in 2011, several police chiefs said 'We have their images' (this was in lieu of their rioting bodies). Here surveillance stands in for the arrests and crowd control that would have previously been the response to such an outbreak of destruction.

Similarly, local authorities send out CCTV cars to video their constituency, driving around with cameras rolling. This is the thing they do to help run-down neighbourhoods; this is also, in a way, the manner in which they keep in touch with their residents. Surveillance becomes the quintessential public service and aid to run-down neighbourhoods, yet it is carried out at arm's length, just as occupying powers sent drones to report on the state of Basra.

The camera also becomes the intermediary in people's relations to one other, functioning as the guarantor of civil and proper behaviour. There are CCTV cameras in schools and care homes, and here the camera is supposed to guard against abuse or failures in these institutions. The officious eye is seen as the basis of restraint and decency in social relations; it is only if they are being watched, apparently, that people will treat each other well. Ethics originates from the restraining presence of the third eye, without which it would be all against all.

The camera is there to spy on the care worker or teacher, to say, 'be careful you are being watched'. But the camera is not only a prosecutor: it is also there for workers' 'protection', for their defence if they should be accused of some misdemeanour by a child or a resident. The proper role of officious surveillance is neither a prosecutor nor defendant, but that of an *intermediary*, the *party through which we relate and which holds us to account*.

(Though it should be noted that profane authorities sometimes assume the eye of the camera as a means of imposing themselves in an institution: one deputy head teacher warned pupils they were being watched on CCTV so should behave, while staff were told that their teaching was being observed so should be of the required standard.)[75]

Searches

The experience of being searched is now entirely commonplace: we are searched at the door of the public building or nightclub, in the street. Football fans are body searched at the entrance to the ground; library readers have their bags searched on the way in. It is no longer only criminal suspects who are asked to empty their pockets and surrender their bags for inspection; it is a daily experience, so common we no longer ask why it is being done.

The search has little practical purpose. Bag searches are rarely thorough: they take a few seconds, zips are opened and the contents rummaged briefly, just moved around a bit. A gun could easily be hidden in the folds of a jumper. Security guards aren't looking for anything in particular; when you ask they say something random like 'spray paint'. These searches have a ritual quality, like a performance, going through the motions of doing a search.

Police stop-and-search powers were supposed to be used to catch terrorists, but after 100,000 stop-and-searches there was not one terrorist conviction.[76] Whatever the function of searches it wasn't to catch terrorists. Instead the search appears to have become part of policing, one of the ways in which local youths are kept in line or 'engaged'. The search joins the beat as a way of projecting police authority in inner-city neighbourhoods.

The role of the search is the disruption of privacy as an end in itself. To officious authority, the citizen is shifty and unknown, he has things hidden in his bags or pockets which are not available to view. Anything private or kept from public view is de facto seen as a threat to authority. The role of the search is to disrupt the personal space that is hidden from view, to intrude upon this space of autonomy, and therefore to neutralise some of its threatening qualities.

Bag searches at the doors of public buildings breach the closed space of the bag and rifle through its contents, fingering lipsticks, diaries, umbrellas. This is an incursion for the sake of an incursion. There is something about the closed bag which is considered an inherent danger, and something about the unzipped and searched bag which is inherently safer. The searched bag has been disrupted and breached, and it is on this basis that it can be judged to be 'safe'.

So the search functions as a boundary to institutions, a condition for entry. In the past, searches at public libraries would occur on the way out, if at all, to check you weren't stealing books. Now one is searched at the door, before one is admitted.[77] The search marks the institution's boundary with the public world and is part of a requirement for admission, like a purification ritual at the door of the temple. The search transforms an unknown and shifting citizenry into something that has been touched by officialdom and is therefore more of a known quantity.

People just wandering around the streets could be anyone; once they are searched they have been officially noted and have submitted something of themselves. They have given their name and address, lifted their arms in surrender, emptied pockets and bags, had trouser legs and torso patted down. The person has been disrupted in going about their business, their autonomy has been violated. It is because of this violation that they are seen to go on their way less of a threat.

Some searches are biochemical: random drugs tests are instituted at the doors of clubs, swabbing club-goers' hands and clothes for traces of illegal substances; some schools in America and Australia subject their students to drug tests.[78] This is not the most efficient manner of deterring drug use, but rather a way to have people offer up their things for chemical analysis, to say, 'come this way please, give me your hands'. The drug test is a projection of authority: the person is tested, swabbed, subjected to a laboratory procedure.

Sniffer dogs jump up at people in train stations and airport queues, searching for traces of prohibited substances. There is no warning and no permission is asked. The person backs to a wall while the dog leaps up at them, running its nose up clothing and around bags while the officer stands there impassively. Because the search is by an animal there is no human encounter, no need for words of warning or explanation. There is no possibility to question or refuse the search: it is over in a second, like a bag snatch. This sudden terroristic search is like a public-order exercise, a warning that sends a frisson of tension around the room once people realise what is happening.

Databases/vetting/reporting

States have always collected information on their populations (from the Domesday Book to the Census) but before this tended to be restricted to vital statistics such as population structure or wealth holdings, for taxation or economic planning.

Now the collection of data is a much more expansive activity. Often the officious answer to any social problem or concern (child abuse, child neglect, illegal immigration or abduction) is to put everybody on a database and institute mass reporting procedures. The sheer quantity of information is fetishised, as if the mass of data could alone ensure the desired policy end.

The officious instinct to build databases appears in unexpected locations, on local as well as central government initiative. Prisons built databases of prison visitors;[79] pubs and clubs built databases on their punters,[80] including fingerprints and reports of rowdy behaviour so that drinkers could be banned at a stroke from all the pubs in town. There were New Labour programmes to place all children, and all 11 million adults working with children, onto separate databases and to monitor them for any signs of risk.[81]

The database functions as the transmutation of the public into a binary and computerised form which can be recognised by officialdom. The database is an abstraction from people in all their complexity and reality, and their transposition into the abstracted form of 'data'. People become numbers or an entry in a system, with logged reports or characteristics.

This public-as-data was characteristic of totalitarian regimes: the Stasi 'card' system, for example, vast rooms within which the population was catalogued and ordered, itemised on cards, illustrating the relationship of a person to other people, represented by other cards. But the card system was allied with a systematic use of force: information was squeezed out of people and used to incriminate and incarcerate. Now databases are built and maintained at vast expense but almost without anybody thinking about how they will be used. The gathering and categorisation of data is seen as an inherently worthy activity. Once people are on a database it is assumed that they are denatured of criminal or dangerous elements.

The public has two relationships to the database: reporting and vetting.

First, a duty of *reporting*: a recording and passing on information about incidents involving oneself or others. For example, schools are supposed to log and report 'prejudiced' incidents, which includes primary-school children's playground insults such as 'Milky Way', 'Mars Bar' or 'broccoli head'.[82] The responsible teacher takes notes, recording exactly what was said and the context, then fills in a form ('child A called child B...') and posts it to the local authority. The local authority then files the forms and produces statistics year to year for the number of 'racist' or 'sexist' incidents in its schools.

The sheer act of filling in forms, sending them to a higher authority who then logs them in a file and a database: this is in itself a socially responsible activity. If a school does not report incidents then this is seen as a sign that they are ignoring prejudice.[83]

Reporting is the act of responsible citizens, passing information up the chain so it can be included in databases. When you are faced with a possible case of abuse or sexual harassment, the advice is always: 'report it'. Ensure that there are 'procedures for reporting, incident forms that can be filled in and posted to a 'designated person' and then subjected to later evaluation. Reporting is a replacement for action, or rather it becomes the action. The action is not to do something about it but to convert the incident into the form of data, 'passing on concerns' and 'logging incidents' in a formalised manner.

When there is intervention, it is triggered not by professional judgement but by an automated procedure. The New Labour child database ContactPoint was supposed to allow professionals to 'flag' their concerns about a child, and after three flags an intervention would be triggered.[84] Barring decisions for those working with children are similarly automated: case workers allot risk weightings of between one and five for various lifestyle factors, and if someone receives two fours, or one five, they are barred.[85] When the state acts it is not the result of professional judgement but as the triggered outcome of algorithm: computer says act. As a result, it appears that the database algorithms obtain an autonomous power, deciding people's fate by an obscure and authorless logic.

The second public relationship to the database is that of *vetting*. Vetting is the process by which you are compared to your entry on the database; a check is run to find out what data comes back. There have been criminal-records checks for decades, but these played a largely technical role alongside personal references and qualifications, to indicate whether someone was suited to a particular professional position. Now the running of a check is given an existential meaning: whether you are a good person and can be trusted. People say with pride that they have a 'clean criminal-records check', which means a clean data entry: there is nothing on me, no blots on my character.

This officious way of treating the public has become internalised, and people start to see their own private lives as consisting of 'data'. One of the ways in which people object to surveillance is to say 'I don't want anyone to access my data'. Here they see their own uniqueness – their personal characteristics, biometric or intimate – already in the abstracted form as statistics that are part of a dataset. The resistance to a database occurs not as a defence of the sanctity of the self, of private relationships or activities, but as an insistence on the private right to one's data. This shows how officiousness has spread into people's very souls even in their resistance against it.

Biometrics

Biometric surveillance such as fingerprints, DNA or face recognition is the cutting-edge area of modern surveillance. Some universities have instilled fingerprint or facial-recognition systems for registering their students at lectures,[86] and until recently artists visiting the UK for collaborations had to be fingerprinted before they could be granted a visa.[87] Some nurseries fingerprint their visitors,[88] while US schoolchildren are fingerprinted before they can claim free school lunches.[89]

In the possession of fingerprints there is an illusion of the possession and control of citizenry, as if once border officials have visitors' fingerprints on file there is no way they can skip their visa. For institutions, the taking of fingerprints symbolises security, discipline, incorporation. Surveillance is seen as an antidote to social disorder and criminality: the taking of fingerprints is a pacifying and neutralising activity.

There is a desire on the part of the officious state to be *certain* about people's identity, for there to be no room for questions. Uncertainty about somebody's identity is not merely an oddity or inconvenience but a threat to authority. It messes up the files.

Biometrics appears to offer a definitive answer, for each individual to be numbered as their fingerprint, DNA, or some other unchangeable vital statistic. While social identity is shifting and uncertain – people can change their name, their job, their appearance – biological identity appears firm and graspable. The use of biometrics reflects the officious state's desire for a definitive categorisation of its citizenry, for everybody to be catalogued and numbered.

It is striking that biometrics focuses on people in their most passive aspect. Stasi surveillance was obsessed with people's activities and associations: what they had done and with whom.

Now the citizen is categorised as a bare life form, as fingerprints, DNA, irises, face shapes. This immanent form of existence becomes our 'real identity' on the database. The citizen as reduced to biological organism is denatured and made safe: they are an unchanging given *body*. They do not make and change themselves but are simply a numbered thing in the world.

The role of surveillance: shadow social life

Taken together this surveillance creates a *shadow social life*: every event and every person gains its mirror image in an estranged, bureaucratic form. Every event becomes a flicker on a screen; every person becomes an item on a database; groups are collated by their fingerprints, names, addresses. The unintelligible, ungraspable citizenry is converted into bureaucratic form, into the language of data and computerised images.

A belief in the primacy of the paper world is characteristic of estranged bureaucracies that seem to generate policy out of themselves. Aleksandr Solzhenitsyn's novel *The First Circle* describes how Stalinist elites were more concerned with whether an event was recorded 'on paper' than whether it actually happened. The secret police would get to know somebody 'by their files' before they got to know them in person: the person would be interpreted through their files and not the other way around.

This doubling of social reality into a bureaucratic form was critiqued by Marx in his work on Hegel. He said that the realm of bureaucratic formality is taken for the real content of social life: 'the bureaucracy is the formal mind of the state', which 'makes its formal aims its content' and 'is obliged to present what is formal for the content and the content for what is formal'. Social life therefore takes on a double meaning in the bureaucratic realm, an estranged reflection which is taken for its essence: 'everything has a double meaning, one real and one bureaucratic, just as

81

knowledge is double, one real and one bureaucratic (and the same with the will). A real thing, however, is treated according to its bureaucratic essence, according to its otherworldly, spiritual essence.'[90]

So it is for the officious state. The reality of independent social life, people going about their business, appears for it as threatening and unknown. When this population is converted into a data form the public seems to exist as a discernible and graspable phenomenon. Surveillance is the process of converting a people into a bureaucratic form, arranging their specific features into various boxes. A person or an event then has a 'double meaning, one real and one bureaucratic'.

Once converted, however, it is the bureaucratic meaning which is taken for the reality. The situation appears upside down. For the officious state, these forms and indices of bureaucratic shadow social life become the reality, and events and people the mere reflection. It is the shadow social life that exists and is real. If somebody is not on a database, do they really exist? If there is no image of the event did it really happen?

The forms of collected data start to structure social life, to determine how a person is treated in reality. People start to organise themselves according to their data entry. For example, groups of volunteers at children's events have been given different colour t-shirts or sashes according to whether they were criminal-records checked.[91] The event is then structured around levels of database clearance: volunteers who have not been vetted cannot help with toilet duty or be alone with a child. People are organised not according to their actual capacities, or what is known of them as individuals, but according to their files.

Those with a flawed data entry as the result of a minor event or bureaucratic error can find themselves barred from jobs, education or bars. Football fans can be placed on a database of 'risk fans' on the basis of police suspicions that they may engage in disorder, or even on the basis of associating with another 'risk fan' (such as drinking in the same pub or sharing a car together). The fan would then be treated differently by police if they were involved in a minor incident: once on the database they become a different category of citizen.[92]

Similarly, one lady was ejected from a London bar for being drunk, then found herself blocked from a different bar on the same ID-sharing database several months later when her ID came up red.[93] An unremarkable drunken incident had been converted into data and transposed into something very different. Thereafter she is treated according to her data entry: a now respectable and sober person is treated not as she is but 'according to her bureaucratic essence'.

Cameras – the public

The third-party intermediary of the camera has also become part of popular culture, one of the ways in which people relate to and come to know each other. This shows again how officiousness is not merely enforced from above but develops spontaneously in the interstices of social life.

Citizens assume the position of the CCTV control room, taking the eye of authority and watching other people. In the past there were cases of people hacking into CCTV cameras, now there are sites where you can watch CCTV cameras and report misdemeanours for which there is a reward. In reality, community vigilance is weak, and people often look the other way in cases of misbehaviour, vandalism or assault, yet vigilance is carried out with enthusiasm through the intermediary of the security camera.

This shows people's estrangement from one another: the voyeuristic relationship between watcher and watched is a relationship at its barest level, without touching. In every voyeuristic relationship one party acts, the other watches, there is a spy and a spied upon. To relate through the camera is not to experience others directly but only through an estranged other eye.

Where watchers express themselves it is through the manipulation of the watched, by voting people out of the *Big Brother* house or off the celebrity island. Here viewers take the role not of fellow citizens but of a public authority to powerless subjects who can be manipulated at will: one day the lights can be turned out, another the alcohol taken away or a person ejected. In a way the watchers play the role of officious authority in relationship to their fellow citizens, as a pleasure and a sport.

As the format progresses this manipulative aspect comes more to the fore. *Big Brother* tasks that used to look like team-building exercises became geared towards humiliation or the destruction of an individual's distinguishing features (a vain man is asked to cut off his curly locks, a timid woman to do a bungee jump).

Yet the camera is experienced not as an intrusion, but as a validation or realisation of the life of an individual. From the late-90s there were cases where people sought to expose themselves on camera, putting webcams in their bedrooms, showing both the mundane and explicit parts of private life. The 'lifecasting' gave the life its form and value. This shows the weakened role of social affirmation and recognition from family, peer groups, authority figures, which are replaced by the sheer exposure and revelation of the self to the impersonal eye of the camera.

The camera, then, represents not just the eye of the state, but of the social itself. This is not a real social in all its substance and variety, but something more like the *officious-social*: the public as transmuted into a blank, surveying and meddling authority, whose affirmation of individuals is at the same time their eclipse.

7

Crime and punishment

The ban

The red sign with a slash-through line has come to define the character of public spaces. The entrance of every public space is announced with large red signs saying what cannot be done within it: no smoking on the platform, no hoodies, no helmets, no cycling. The character of public space is given by its specific menu of restrictions, the things that cannot be done.

The meaning of the ban is legislation as mere restriction. It is legislation that creates a slash through social life, which puts up a barrier and says merely, 'this cannot be done'. This is not legislation that seeks to provide services, or organise social life on a more rational basis: it is the creation of a no-go zone.

The ban is the embodiment of an interfering, disapproving authority, which finds its raison d'être in interfering in other people's habits. The officious officer will look out their window at children skateboarding or playing in the fountain, and think: they shouldn't be doing that. The following week a sign will appear: no skateboarding, no bathing in the fountain. Over time an increasing number of activities will be added.

It is through this sort of restriction that the officious state defines itself and makes its presence felt. For the officious state, there is rarely a good reason not to ban things, and lifestyle bans are posed as the answer to every social problem or ethical failing. If young people are being disrespectful the answer is to ban them from spitting or wearing hoods or low-slung trousers. If there are street alcoholics, the answer is to ban them from entering the park or to ban drinking in public.

Here the banning of a habit – the symbol or emblem of social problems – becomes the primary way in which the state can affect society, and replaces substantive interventions. The ban becomes a public service.

Increasingly, the lifestyle ban defines state authority. One of the few things that a politician can do at a stroke is to ban something or other, which is why a ban is often the first act of a new regime or government. The first act of the London mayor Boris Johnson was to ban drinking on the Tube, a benign habit that had been largely restricted to tired commuters and snoozy drunks. The role of the ban was not to deal with a social problem but to announce the new regime, to at a stroke effect a change in the life of the city.

This ideological role explains the excessive passion with which politicians propose bans on some minor habit or practice. Various smoking bans have been described as 'making history'; councillors seeking bans on spitting are gripped by an ecumenical zeal. The parliamentary houses of France and Belgium pulled out all rhetorical flourishes to bring through bans on burqas.[94] In particular, the Belgian government was in a state of dissolution, all lawmaking had ceased, yet politicians managed to come together for an emergency session to prohibit this rare form of women's headwear.

It is through lifestyle prohibition that the state can make its own statement of values. And so French republicanism is increasingly defined against the burqa, without which perhaps it would lose all definition. The Spanish state of Catalonia banned both bullfighting, the habit associated with the rule of Madrid, and the burqa, associated with Muslim immigrants. So the Catalonian principle is defined: not-Madrid, and not-Islam. By prohibiting the cultural practices of others one makes one's own statement of principle.

The ban, therefore, bears the weight of state ideological definition and legislative capacity. The ban doesn't reflect society but serves ideological needs intrinsic to the state or those in authority. This is distinct from the traditional role of bans which, as Emile Durkheim says, are immanent in everyone's consciousness: the prohibited act 'offends the strong, well defined states of the collective consciousness'.[95]

Bans often appear to be disconnected from social life, slapped down from above without reason or warning. Overnight a local council brings through a no-dog zone on the local beach where everyone walks their dogs. The ban violates common and accepted usage, sometimes targeting the primary public use of a space. Cultural icons are violated by the strike-through line. One town banned kissing on the train platform (the very place you are supposed to kiss),[96] while Rome banned bathing in the fountain which was used for the bathing scene in *La Dolce Vita*.[97]

Today's officious bans are distinguished by their pettiness and lack of unifying theme. There is none of the moral singularity of previous bans such as Prohibition. The officious ban will target the symbol of a problem, or something associated with a problem: they would rather issue 100 petty bans than one proper one.

There is no prohibition of alcohol, but bans on public drinking in parks, low-cost alcohol, drinks promotions such as 'happy hour', 'sexy' cocktail names, adverts which associate alcohol with 'sexual or social success'. There is no ban on smoking, but bans on 10-packs, smoking in public places, branded packaging, the display of cigarettes in shops. Outside pubs there are lines drawn on the ground behind which drinkers must stand; there are lines near the entrance to buildings which smokers must not cross. There are even 'smoking boxes' painted out on the pavement.

Never has so much attention been paid to the *appearance* of tobacco or alcohol: the images on the packaging, the position and location of the display, the product name, the exact positions in which they may be consumed. Never did authorities tell smokers exactly where they should stand.

The extension of bans doesn't favour one group over another, or enforce a strict code, but extends the officious state into the nooks and crannies of social life, as the ordainer of acceptability and the ever-present presiding judge.

Busybodies and open-ended powers

The new criminal law is not composed of precisely delimited powers or definitions of crime. The new officials are not 'servants of the law'. Instead, law or powers are described as 'tools' which allow them to do what they want to do: to stop and search, to move on, to confiscate, to ban. In policy circles a new power will be described as a 'great new tool': the official decides what they want to do then looks for a power that allows them to do it. The official is the subject, the law an object in their hands which they apply for their own purposes.

More precisely, law is described as a 'tool*kit*': a new power is described as a 'great addition to the toolkit' or a 'valuable part of a menu of options'. What is valued is that officials have a free hand: that in any given circumstance they have plenty of options to choose from, that they never find themselves at a loss or want to do something and cannot. This concern with *choice* of action shows how the criminal law has pursued the freedom of the official, their freedom of movement and action, as an end in itself. This is why the use of powers is also described as 'creative'.

Open-ended powers have been drawn up with little thought as to how these powers will be used. The expansion of powers becomes the primary criminal-justice strategy and the answer to a wide variety of social problems. Independent social life is seen as the realm of latent criminality: anything hidden, anything free or unregulated, is latently criminal. By the same accounts the official's intervention (or realm of intervention) has the civilising force of anti-crime or crime-prevention strategy.

The confidence in officials is not specific, justified on the basis of their personal qualities or the quality of their institution.

Instead, there is a blind faith in the non-specific 'official' of no particular institution, only because they represent the negation of civic life. It is the negativity towards civil society which drives a blind faith in power-bearing officials.

There has been an expansion of civil powers to 'order'. Here state power is detached from the criminal law – from the enforcement of general laws which are violated in the criminal act – and becomes a personalised mechanism for directing the behaviour of particular individuals. The powers to order are quintessential busybody powers, a matter of meddling and not law enforcement.

In the UK, there are antisocial-behaviour orders (ASBOs),[98] control orders (which impose conditions on somebody suspected of terrorism), crime-prevention orders, sexual offences-prevention orders, dispersal orders (to remove people from a locality), parenting orders (which could require parents to go to counselling), football-banning orders (which ban an individual from attending football matches). In the USA there are a variety of orders which can ban individuals from particular areas of town, including private property, such as parks exclusion orders, stay out of area orders and trespass admonishments.[99] In Australia there are prohibited-behaviour orders.

Once an order is issued it has the force of law: for that individual, it becomes a criminal offence to do whatever is prohibited in the order, such as to cross a particular street, to use a particular word or to wear a cap. The order represents the breakdown of the criminal law as a standardised and predictable set of rules for the conduct of social life. Each order is a person-alised intervention by the state in the conduct of an individual.

(In the UK there has been a development of a pre-order infra-structure, based on the contract – good-behaviour contract, parenting contract – where a person signs a contract with state authorities to behave in a particular way. This is not really a contract but a series of conditions imposed on the individual, behaviours they must manifest or avoid, and if they violate the contract then the state will move to the next stage of making an order.)

Orders become a shadow justice system, a parallel system for the use of state power which is founded on a quite different basis. These contracts and orders total tens of thousands each year. There have been 25,000 ASBOs in the UK and there are 25,000 parenting contracts each year. In the city of Seattle there are 10,000 trespass orders issued each year.[100]

The criminal law itself starts to approximate the system of orders, with the deliberate creation of offences so broad as to allow the law to be invoked in almost any case. The definition of a crime is designed to be a catch-all that allows for orders to be issued in specific cases, rather than a specific description of behaviour meriting criminal sanction. Sexual-offences law, for example, means that almost everybody has committed a sexual offence: it is a crime for a 15-year-old boy to kiss his girlfriend of the same age.[101] Law professor Andrew Ashworth says that this was a relatively conscious attempt to give prosecutors the widest latitude possible: 'prosecutors don't like there to be things they cannot prosecute'.[102] Similarly, UK councils have created laws prohibiting 'any object which could cause harm', 'standing in a group of two or more unless waiting at a bus stop', and 'shouting'.[103] These offences cannot be enforced with any consistency, nor are they intended to be: the aim is to provide a broad remit which allows orders to be issued for people to move on or discontinue their activity.

The US legal academic William J Stuntz argues: 'When legal doctrine makes everyone an offender, the relevant offences have no meaning independent of law enforcers' will. The formal rule of law yields to the functional rule of official discretion.'[104] The will of the official becomes in itself the law.

The expansion of crime

The officious state representative is relatively uninterested in actual crime, in actual violations of person or property. They are much more interested in the grey areas, in the areas of social life *around* crime – before crime, or related to crime.

They are not interested in bag-snatching per se but in the conditions within which bag-snatching might occur, including elements of social life such as alcohol, crowds, music, the presence of homeless people, swearing. They are keen to 'nip it in the bud' (to intervene before crime has happened) or to target areas of life which they believe are associated with crime.

The intervention is not a defined response to a defined criminal act: it becomes a project of intervening in social life, which is relatively detached from any criminal offences. Officials intervene in 'drinking cultures' which are 'associated with criminal activity', with measures such as prohibiting public drinking or banning homeless people from the park. Or they ban adverts or films which they claim to be 'associated with sexual offences'.

In the USA, officers have wide-ranging powers to confiscate property associated with criminal activity: they have confiscated a woman's car which had been used by her husband for kerb-crawling, and a building which was used by one of the tenants for dealing drugs.[105] The relatedness of an item of property to a criminal act means that it is tainted, declared an outlaw, and can be seized, even if the owner had no role in the crime.

Innocent and anodyne parts of social life are claimed to be 'associated with crime' or to 'cause a downward spiral of crime'. The Association of Chief Police Officers made this claim of live music, saying that 'Live music always acts as a magnet in whatever community it is being played. It brings people from outside that community and others who come and having no connection locally behave in a way that is inappropriate, criminal and disorderly.'[106] Similar claims have been made of drinking, busking, large crowds, even lost-cat posters (Canterbury City Council says that posters of all kinds 'help give the impression of urban decay' and cause a 'spiral of crime').[107]

It becomes an anti-crime strategy for officialdom to seek a social life that is inhibited, quiet, clean, without conflict or unexpected events or high emotions ('cleaner, safer, greener' is the policy phrase). This was first seen in New York mayor Giuliani's 'zero tolerance', the point at which it became an anti-crime strategy to prevent people putting their bags on the seat in the subway.

There are new officious crimes: it becomes a crime to drink in public, walk your dog in a particular park, hand out leaflets or busk without a licence. This represents a return to the idea of crime as latent in crowds and sociability, in unregulated activity or in high emotion.

Summary: punishment

The classic officious punishment is the on-the-spot fine. Fifteen years ago there were almost no on-the-spot fines in the UK (below 11,000), and only for a limited series of parking offences, now they are a normal and everyday experience (over 200,000).[108]

There are fines for misdemeanours such as: walking your dog in the wrong area, putting items in the wrong rubbish bin, messy gardens, spitting, unlicensed leafleting or busking, truancy, swearing or 'offensive' behaviour. In Australia, New South Wales police issue $500 fines for swearing.[109]

The on-the-spot fine is the officious penalty par excellence: it is the parking ticket, the slap on the wrist for a minor offence after which the official walks on their way. It requires none of the discipline of prosecution, nor the moral authority of a telling-off. The on-the-spot fine is amoral: it is issued in a few seconds and can be paid online like a gas bill. It can be issued and received with a shrug of the shoulders. The role of the fine is to 'discharge liability for the offence', which means that it is a semi-punishment, a paper punishment of which everybody washes their hands.

It is striking how the on-the-spot fine is now the de facto answer to such a broad range of incidents. First, in some cases it replaces prosecution and trial for criminal offences: magistrates complain that theft and assault are being increasingly dealt with by spot fines rather than being summoned before their benches.

Secondly, fines are being used to deal with social problems that would have been dealt with through social-services interventions, such as fines for truancy or for street drinkers. It is through coercive interventions that councils and police say that they are 'helping' the homeless: some councils have imposed fines for rough sleeping, others for begging or 'aggressive begging'.[110] Now an average London street drinker gets a fine every couple of weeks and alcohol confiscated every few days.[111] Such petty punishments become street drinkers' dominant experience of state services.

Finally, fines are used to deal with impoliteness or moral failings (swearing, rudeness, spitting) which would have been dealt with through public disapproval or institutional discipline. Here the officious parking ticket replaces the self-regulation of civil society. Indeed, it is now commonly thought that an official issuing fines is the only way in which bad habits can be disciplined or rules enforced. Many cannot imagine any way in which young people could be persuaded to stop spitting or swearing through social pressure. Social pressure 'doesn't work', they say, the only answer is to call in the wardens with fining slips.

The parking ticket therefore takes over areas once occupied by law and order, state services, and social mores. It expands to subsume both the court trial and informal self-regulation of civil society, with the seeming belief that society can be regulated and held together by this ever-growing pile of £75 and £80 tickets.

The new criminal justice in context

Taken together, these changes represent a new kind of criminal law, a change in the basis of punitive powers. Modern criminal law is traditionally grounded in the unit of the autonomous individual: this is the unit from which all its forms are derived, including forms of legal procedure and definitions of crime. The definition of a crime in a modern state was: the individual act which wilfully harms or violates the liberty of another person.[112] Whereas customary injunctions are based only on the question of obedience or disobedience, a legal code is based on the elements of responsibility, harm, and equivalence.

Officious criminal law detaches state power and punishment from its origins in the unit of the autonomous individual. This expansion of state power is not an assertion of state interests, or the interests of a clique against society. It is notable that there are no new branches of law explicitly defending interests of state. There is no equivalent of treason or heresy laws, no new sedition or show trials. There is no new inquisition court or Star Chamber, no legal sphere in which the state rules as subject and society as defendant cowers prostrate before it.

Criminal justice has been detached from its origins, but has not been replaced with any alternative logic. Punitive powers float unhinged on the top of society, without principles governing their use. The idea that law is a 'tool' suggests it is merely a detached coercive instrument, lying around, which can be picked up and used for this or that. There is nothing in the instrument which suggests that it need be used for a particular purpose. Its quality comes only from what it can 'do' (i.e. the specific restrictions it can induce); the question of its use is left entirely open. The means of coercion have become separated from any system governing the use of that coercion, which is to say from social relations and determination.

Law has collapsed into the subjectivity of officials: there is nothing standing over their heads, judging and holding them to account. Law is immediately one with the exercise of coercion; it is simply whatever is backed up with sanctions. Coercive powers do not come with the sharp specification of legitimate and illegitimate use, such that every coercive power or law has as its inverse a domain of right.

Criminal law starts to become random in its operations. People don't know when they are committing an offence or when or why they will be picked upon. They are often surprised when they are fined by busybodies; they had no idea they were committing an offence. They didn't know that the park was a no-dog zone or that it was a crime to drink on the beach. As the American lawyer Philip K Howard argues, the law seems designed to catch you out, and on a certain level people start to accept the notion that most things are probably a crime and they no longer understand the law.[113]

Punishment becomes a fitful and erratic business, reversing the trend of millennia which was towards a greater systematisation and standardisation of punishment in order to fit the crime. From the earliest codes, which laid down the punishments corresponding to each criminal act; to the development of forms of trial to establish the facts of a case; to the development of criminal codes or systems of precedent; to the creation of an impartial system of judges without personal ties or allegiance to the sovereign: the tendency over time has been the increasing predictability of criminal justice. In primitive societies 'punitive reactions' are 'free from procedural formality or rule', says Weber, but 'A slow subjection to rules occurred'.[114] The social order came increasingly to rely upon 'legal legitimation', with a growing systematisation of legal propositions and coherence of legal doctrine.[115]

Whim is now returning as the mainstay of criminal justice, and punishment is again becoming summary, random and pecuniary. Law is no longer a 'system', says Harold J Berman, but a 'fragmented mass of ad hoc decisions and conflicting rules' and 'basically an instrument of the state'.[116]

The relation between state and society is inverted. In classic liberal law, civil society is assumed to be free, and the state is restrained by the law. In the officious state, civil society is restrained by red tape and bans, and the state is made free through the law. The essence of officious law is only: restriction for citizens, freedom for the state. This represents the formalisation of society and the informalisation of the state.

The corruption of punishment

Inasmuch as there is a systematic interest beneath this dynamic, it is of the most erratic and privatised character, the basest and shallowest form of self-interest on the part of officials.

There is a degree of corruption in Anglo-Saxon criminal justice which has not been seen for several centuries. Because the use of power is neither governed by law, nor by systematic elite interests, the door is left open for punishment to be driven by personal material interests of officials themselves.

The two main forms of officious corruption come from: first, fines; and second, targets.

Fines and payoffs

The on-the-spot fine provides a base pecuniary motive to punishment. Some council departments now subsist in large part from their fines income, meaning that an environmental department issuing fines starts to have a private, parasitic interest, apart from the public interest of the local authority. The department becomes a private business with its own circular and self-interested economy: wardens go out to issue fines, to pay for more wardens, to go out and issue more fines. The fine is the way in which they earn their salary; they subsist from their power to punish.

Such local authority departments become interested not in the most serious offences but in those which can yield the most fines, which are generally the minor offences which are most common and easiest to catch (the very easiest to catch are the cases where the person does not know they are doing anything wrong). The fine is no longer a necessary form of punishment to encourage lawful behaviour: officials need to fine, and so need the offence, and if there are no offences they need to invent them in order that they can continue to issue fines.

Wardens start to engage in low-life practices, tailing or following people, hiding around corners, chasing or intimidating them. Their relationship to the public is one of overt hostility and economic parasitism. One warden described the situation: 'We spent our time stalking people who were smoking cigarettes... we were filming them. I have seen colleagues chase behind people to issue tickets, go into shops after people and take them out... They [his employers] started pushing for any sort of ticket.'[117]

This corrupt aspect is even more pronounced when councils employ private companies to fine on a commission basis, as around 15 UK councils currently do (collectively these are responsible for over half of all fines issued).[118] When a council contracts these wardens they are basically calling in the mercenaries against their own residents. Perversely, the local authority often sees the number of fines as a question of 'performance', citing an increase in fines as an 'improvement in performance'. The fine – a tax and drain upon the public – is transposed into a form of public service and a measure of state efficiency.

In the USA open-ended confiscation powers have been used to bring in the budget for police departments or to settle personal scores. Cases abound of people being stopped and in effect robbed by the police, with the officer seizing cash or valuables from a car in lieu of a court case.[119] This has been called a new age of 'robber barons', bare-faced theft by the authorities which leaves property rights in a tenuous position.

What is significant is the base and erratic quality of this parasitic punishment. There have been previous societies in which elite corruption and rent-seeking were carried out in a systematic manner, such as systems of patronage or local pork-barrel politics. In these cases, payments were based on self-interest but they also regulated and contributed to social order. By contrast, the self-interest of officious punishment is privatised and random, working not to social order but to the anarchy of robber barons or pirates. In failed states power belongs to any man with a gun; in officious states power lies with any person with an official badge that endows the power to fine.

This has been shown by several instances of conmen posing as wardens. They wore fake uniforms and badges, watching the public for minor misdemeanours for which they issued a 'fine' and marched them to the cash machine.[120] Councils and the private security company criticised this fraud, but the uncomfortable fact is that the conmen revealed the actual substance of their public service to be nothing more than private profiteering. The conmen's actions were not substantially different in content or consequences to those of the authorised officers. In both cases, wardens were looking for people to fine in order to earn a salary. The criminal act showed the truth of state activity.

Targets

The second form of officious corruption is the target or league table. Here officials will issue punishments or otherwise behave in a manner that enables them to meet their targets or to rise up the league table. The target is, in effect, a form of bureaucratic currency: the official is acting in such a way as to win themselves more points, a pseudo-currency issued by the state bureaucracy. More points equal more budget, or a promotion, or some other favourable treatment.

The assumption behind the target is that officials are only self-interested, and it is through targets and other artificial bureaucratic mechanisms that they can be encouraged to act as part of a collective body. Some of these targets nominally measure public goods (police effectiveness at prosecution, for example) but in fact they transform these into bureaucratic measures, which are then sought without regard to their effect on social life.

There are cases of police officers issuing fines to kids for minor misdemeanours in order to meet their target for 'offences brought to justice'. Here is an account of the incentive systems:

> One North Wales division awards "points" to officers depending on how they deal with a crime. A Penalty Notice for Disorder scores 20 points compared to submitting intelligence for which you receive "nil points". Sanction detections score five points if accompanied by an arrest and officers must get four a month to reach their target. In Essex, an inspector sets the number of sanction detections they expect their officers, including probationers, to attain each week. In some forces, bonuses are paid to BCU commanders who achieve performance indicators and in one force at least, commanders can financially reward junior officers who achieve the best results.[121]

The police officer here is not so different to the private security guard paid on commission for every fine: both are driven by a need to get so many 'hits' per week and view the public as a source of punishment slips.

Targets can also mean that potential crimes are ignored. Some London police forces have pressured women to drop rape allegations because rape is a crime that is difficult to prove and leads to lower success rates.[122] The public interest that claims be properly investigated is passed over for the bureaucratic measure of 'success'.

The role of the target is to transform the relationship between public servant and public into a relationship between the self-interested official and the state bureaucracy. The target undermines the public-service ethos, pushing public servants towards the inhuman and alienated measures of the state. The operations of a public service start to be moulded by the standards and measures drawn from the shadow world of bureaucracy, rather than by the substance of the useful work performed.[123]

8

State and society, freedom and coercion

The categories of state and civil society are ceasing to exist as principled distinctions. There are now in principle few parts of social life which cannot be touched by official regulation. Of course, there are still some independent areas of life but these are not systematically maintained and could be breached at any moment.

The questions that were classically decided within civil society, such as questions of etiquette or basic comportment, are now mediated through public authority. Croydon Council in London planned to prohibit 'rowdy and/or inconsiderate behaviour' and issue fines for the offence. When a council prohibits 'inconsiderate behaviour' then there is really no domain left for civic life. The code or formal prohibition supplants the relations between people: it seems to be the thing that makes their relation possible and brings them into relation. Custom or common practice has no substantive being; all that remains is the external formal injunction.

This dynamic has developed within the public itself. It is not uncommon for people to see coercive tools of criminal law as their mouthpiece, as the way of sanctifying their particular view on the world or their likes and dislikes. The coercive machinery provides a mechanism through which debate is conducted or relations mediated. Any claim to universality now involves an element of coercion. To claim to superiority or universal relevance means only to be *enforced* as such. The universal cannot exist except through imposition.

The only legitimate free action is the action of coercion against others. This amounts to the legitimacy of the act of coercion as opposed to the illegitimacy of the act of freedom. The ethic of the day is: freedom to coerce! Freedom for badged officials, however lowlife, whatever their actions. Even the basest and most disreputable official is seen as safe and civilised, while by the same accounts the most respectable free act is seen as unsafe and illegitimate. One cannot be free in oneself or act for oneself; the only legitimately free act is to take on the mantle of the busybody and act against others.

Under officiousness, informal relations are mediated through a formal mechanism and the most everyday things become 'special', no longer the free action of the owners but something done with supervision. The most everyday things, too, become coerced, done under a kind of duress. When university students sign a consent form before going to bed, even the most intimate moment attains a coercive element, as something that is overseen and with potential sanctions implied.

Lenin argued that the existence of special procedures and formal coercion was the result of the contradictions in social relations under capitalism. The Bolsheviks imagined that under Communist society special coercive procedures would disappear even from areas such as criminal justice. With the transcendence of social contradictions, there would be no 'special machine' or 'special apparatus of repression' and crime would be dealt with 'with the same simplicity and ease with which any crowd of civilised people... separate a couple of fighters or stop an act of violence against a woman'.[124]

Now the realms in which people can conduct their relations with 'simplicity and ease' have contracted dramatically, and the capacities once assumed by 'any crowd of civilised people' have become the exclusive property of specially qualified officials. Now the 'special machine' stretches its reach in some cases even into the bedroom.

Therefore, there is a contemporary radicality to the uncoerced, unmediated relation; and there is a radical task of defending the realm of the social against the realm of the official. The existence of free and direct relations is the precondition for the development of more political forms. Jurgen Habermas outlined how the development of the bourgeois public sphere began with the sphere of the private conversation and intimacy within the conjugal family, with salons and letter-writing, and only later moved into the realm of public affairs.[125] There were salons before there were political parties, literary journals before there were political journals.

The officious supervision of everyday life blocks the development of social formations. The restriction of informal relations blocks the development of new social forms that might begin to express public and political interests. The re-establishment of the autonomy of the social sphere is a precursor for developing more popular and democratic forms of politics, including systems of public service and public representation.

It is civil society's capacity for self-mediation which forms the line of distinction and defence against the state. If society is not self-mediating, it ceases to exist as a realm and therefore as a category in everyday life and policy. This means the political project of defending the boundary of civic life: it is the negation of the negation, establishing the value and integrity of the social as set against the realm of officiousness. This is the political project of the expulsion of bureaucratic mediation from the sphere of social life.

9

Opposing officiousness

The conflict of interest between state and society

It is true that the primary cause of officiousness is the vacuum in civic life. It is also true that officiousness has spread throughout society, that it has been adopted spontaneously and become part of how many people relate to one another. And yet we can still say that officiousness is fundamentally part of the state, and is opposed to and in conflict with the interest of society.

The officious citizen is different to the officious official. While the official is acting out something of the quality of being an official, the citizen is acting against their interests. Officiousness is in some ways the pure and natural ideology for officialdom; it is the stripping of the state down to its defining quality of being raised above society with special powers over it. By contrast, for the citizen to talk and act in this way – to use officious language, to call for bans or tell other citizens that 'procedures must be followed' – is the violation of their status as citizen.

A citizen who has adopted officious forms of thought has perverted their relations with others, they have betrayed and silenced themselves. By calling in the state to ban other people's habits they only confirm their own subordination to state authority and their own incapacity. The person calling for the council to ban music on buses is only confirming their own inability to talk to others and to ask them to please turn their music down. By petitioning the third party to act as their intermediary and mouthpiece, they silence themselves.

The objective conflict of interest between state and civil society creates a potential for political conflict. In previous periods the defining political conflicts were between social classes: the plebs and patricians in Rome, aristocracy and bourgeoisie in the 17th and 18th centuries, the bourgeoisie and working classes in the 19th and 20th centuries. The state rose above this conflict, coloured and formed by it, acting as a mediator and enforcer of the interests of the dominant party.

Now there is a new potential conflict of interest opening up between parts of the state structure and civil society. In its officious form, the state becomes a true parasite, usurping social resources for the blocking of social life, charging fees and issuing fines to sap the life force of civil society. It answers only to its own logic and works only for maintenance of its own hostile body.

Therefore, after the decline of social classes and old forms of political conflict we can see potential for a new objective conflict of interest between the officious bureaucracy and society. What is at stake in this conflict is the existence of independent civic life as such.

In this context, the public's annoyance at the intrusions of 'busybodies' has a contemporary radicality. When an official is experienced as a busybody – as an arbitrary invasion into the body of the social, as an interrupter, disrupter, interferer – this suggests a grounding to that social which can be defended. It suggests a potential flashpoint; at this point the social has being. Where someone sees a busybody there is a barricade, there is something authentic to be defended.

Rebellions against officiousness

There are points at which this objective conflict of interest becomes conscious, and the basis for political mobilisation. There are not a large number of these points. Because officiousness is premised upon the weakening of civic life – a social fragmentation and mutual suspicion, and reduction of independence – by definition there will be relatively little resistance to its incursions, and little consciousness of the violation that is taking place. An ideology produced by quiescence by definition faces few barriers.

Yet there are points where officiousness over-reaches itself, where it comes into conflict with a vibrant and self-assured part of social life. There are points at which a regulation or an official tries to stop people doing things they want to do, where the state's disruption and restraint of social life is experienced as an unjustified incursion. These are the points at which protests start, where the objective conflict between officiousness and society is transformed into a form of political action.

Just as officious regulations target all social classes and groups without distinction, so do rebellions against them come from all walks of life. Every form of officious regulation – the ban, surveillance, licence forms, vetting, fines, risk assessments – has at some point come into conflict with a group or individual which experiences it as an unjustified incursion.

Buskers in Leeds and Camden protested against busking licences; music groups organised against 'regulated enter-tainment' licensing; inner-city neighbourhoods in Birmingham covered up their CCTV cameras and called for them to be removed; pub owners protested against council requirements that they video their customers. There were swear-ins to protest against the Australian ban on swearing; drink-ins to protest against the banning of drinking in Berlin's Alexanderplatz; a party against the banning of alcohol on the London Tube. Football supporters protested against bans on 'offensive' chants; dog walkers have marched against bans on dog-walking in parks or on beaches.

Flower arrangers at Gloucester Cathedral resigned in protest when they were asked to complete criminal-records checks, as have other volunteers. Swimmers in Hampstead in London took a legal case defending their right to swim in the early morning without the presence of a lifeguard. Residents of Gloucester defied the council's health-and-safety ban on their annual 'cheese-rolling' competition (where residents roll cheeses and then themselves down a hill).[126]

At each of these points, collective or individual subjectivity came into conflict with the officious state, which was seeking to suppress or restrain it. Here, officiousness is experienced as what is really is: a hostile and negative incursion, a violation of social activity and independence.

What is being asserted in the protest is the essential innocence and competence of social life, the right to autonomous action and self-regulation. This is explicit in some of the campaign slogans: 'photographers not terrorists', 'students not suspects', 'football supporters not criminals'. The group asserts that the innocent majority should not be treated like criminals; they defy the view of social life as suspect, shady and criminal. They assert the norm as innocent: they say, we are just photographers, this is an ordinary thing to do. After the Hampstead swimmers won their case, one 64-year-old swimmer who had been swimming in the ponds for 33 years said: 'We have been fighting for the right to take responsibility for ourselves and that is a right we have won today'.[127] They were fighting for an assertion of their own competence – they are swimmers, they can handle themselves – and also for the right to bear the consequences of their own actions.

It may appear that these issues are 'soft' issues. Matters such as the right to swim in the early morning or the right to drink or take photos in public may not appear to be matters of life and death.

Yet it has always been the case that freedom campaigns were fought through particular questions that did not appear to be matters of life and death. The questions of the right to read the Bible in English, or to say that the wine was not actually the blood of Christ, do not appear to be highly pressing questions compared to issues such as mass hunger or slavery. Yet it was upon such disputes that hereticism and then the Reformation were based, since they contained within them the question of freedom of conscience and people's relationship to the church hierarchy.

English rebels in the Civil War made great play of refusing to take the oath of the King's Star Chamber. What did it matter? It was only an oath, only a few words. Similarly, many often say: what does a criminal-records check or a fingerprint matter? It is only a form; it doesn't hurt or cost that much; if you haven't done anything wrong it should not concern you. Yet within that Star Chamber oath, and within the criminal-records check, is contained the whole question of one's subjection to arbitrary authority, one's submission and unfreedom.

A freedom issue is not only about the concrete thing at stake, but also about the *underlying principle of right or submission contained within that thing*. It is the challenge of political campaigning to bring this underlying principle to light and to consciousness.

Finally, it should be noted that many of these groups protesting against busybody regulations have found allies among more public-spirited state representatives. Oxford councillors stood alongside buskers and homeless people against the council's plan to ban 'non-compliant' busking and rough sleeping; Cambridge councillors took the side of street drinkers forced out of public spaces; musicians and photographers have found parliamentary supporters in both houses. This suggests that the fight against officiousness also involves a conflict between public service and busybody elements within state authorities.

Pointers for the way ahead

These conflicts between different social groups and the officious state have a basis in social interests that other political issues today often appear to lack. In their reactions against officiousness, people want to do something that they are being prevented from doing: the issue is simple and clear. Their demand is only to be granted the space within which to exercise their autonomy, to photograph or busk unmolested and without arduous demands being made of them.

These groups are from different political and social backgrounds, but share a certain libertarianism, a certain independence of spirit and worldview, which is partly a question of character and partly the result of an experience of coming into conflict with officious regulation. It is striking to witness the radicalisation of pensioners who have been fined and humiliated by a private security guard for walking their dog in an unmarked no-dog zone. Their libertarianism is a product of the conflict of interest between their subjective action and the obstructive regulation.

The virtue of these conflicts is that they are grounded in a concrete conflict of interest between particular subjectivity and a particular regulation. However, this is perhaps also their limitation. It is possible for a group to defend their own right to pursue their chosen activity, but support the suppression of some other group or some other activity. People may say that they oppose smoking bans in parks, for example, but agree with alcohol bans because 'I don't drink'; or they may support rights for elderly ladies to walk their dogs in a park, but not for young people to skateboard or homeless people to drink in public.

There is a tendency, therefore, to demand not a right – a general principle, for civil society as a whole – but a privilege for a particular group. Groups often lobby government with the aim of gaining exemption for their particular activity. Their aim is to get a 'by' inserted in the law which would give them special exemption from a general rule. Once they gain this they lose interest in the issue.

Alternatively, if an organisation is regulated and cannot escape, their demand perversely becomes that others be similarly restricted. The Oxford Playhouse theatre was not concerned about the council's leafleting ban (under which student drama societies would have to pay £100 a month for the right to hand out leaflets) because the Playhouse was already restricted from leafleting by their licensing conditions. In fact, the theatre's primary complaint was that although they abided by these conditions and did not leaflet, other theatres in the city did not, and so were therefore at an unfair advantage. The call here is not freedom for all, but equal restrictions for all. A similar sentiment is voiced by street traders who support leafleting licences because they themselves have to buy a licence.

Particularist consciousness has always been a limitation on the development of freedom campaigns. John Locke regretted that different religious sects demanded freedoms and prerogatives for their own group which directly violated the civil rights of others.[128] Such a claim is not actually a claim for freedom at all, but for a privilege.

In feudal England people would petition the king for a licence to trade in a particular article or to publish a particular book. The request was not for free trade, or a free press, but for the granting of a particular privilege or *monopoly*. The individuals granted this privilege were the most conservative and loyal, since they had received the king's grace. It was the licensed printers of the Stationers' Company that went around raiding and smashing the presses of unlicensed printers.

A similar dynamic can be seen today with, for example, gay and Muslim groups competing to ban each other's publications and speakers. Each is seeking not their own freedom, but the right to a monopoly of public opinion. As a result, they endow the state with the authority to legislate on matters of truth and social or cultural mores. The debate is not about freedom, the boundaries between citizens and the state, but about which particular habits are worthy of official recognition and protection.

The process of demanding exemption need not cement the authority of the state, however. If it is merely a demand for autonomy, and not linked to the call for the suppression of other groups, then calls for exemption can be widened and start to establish the principle of freedom across the board. In the period prior to the issuing of Magna Carta, for example, towns purchased privileges of freedoms, which over time became established as a general rule.[129] Similarly, UK musicians obtained a reform of music licensing (an exemption of small music events) which was later extended to other forms of regulated entertainment licensing, similarly freeing dancing, theatre and film.

Our aim should be to start from positions of social interest, concrete conflicts between different groups and the officious state, but for these to become aligned and so to represent a more conscious and universalistic cause, which is the cause of civil society in general. Certainly the main thing to be avoided is particularist groups defending their own 'freedom' directly at the cost of others, which only extends officious authority.

The conflict between officious authority and civil society will mean new contests around new issues and the formation of unfamiliar alliances. The main challenge will be the question of solidarity between different groups within civil society, which, ultimately, is the only force capable of sending the busybodies back behind their curtains.

Endnotes

1. For example, in Lenin's *State and Revolution*, Engels' *Origin of the Family, Private Property and the State*, and Marx's *Critique of Hegel's Philosophy of Right*

2. 'Critique of Hegel's Doctrine of the State', Karl Marx, *Early Writings*, Penguin, 1977, p109

3. 'Folkestone man misses date because of "fag butt police"', *Folkestone Herald*, 28 January 2013

4. For example: 'Woman fined over dropped crisps', *BBC News*, 17 May 2007; 'Disabled boy "faced fine of up to £2,500" for dropping litter from car', *Hull Daily Mail*, 16 March 2014. There have been hundreds of fines issued to pensioners for bird-feeding or walking dogs in the wrong area.

5. 'Bureaucracy', *Essays in Sociology*, Max Weber, Routledge, 2009, p215

6. *Policing Victorian London*, Phillip Thurmond Smith, Greenwood Press, 1985, p40

7. For example, the TaxPayers' Alliance 'non-job of the week': http://www.taxpayersalliance.com/non_job_of_the_week_71 bsqom8x2t6078vs_7egux7nbs

8. *Bin Police Work Overtime*, Manifesto Club briefing document, 14 September 2012

9. 'Couple banned from hanging fairy lights for "health and safety"', *Daily Telegraph*, 11 December 2010

10. Julie Spence, former head of Cambridgeshire Police. Interviewed in *Checking Up*, Josie Appleton, Civitas, October 2014

11. This was the case in my council, Camden.

12. I worked with mothers seeking to overturn a heavily defended photoban at their children's school in Welwyn Garden City: 'Parents seek photo "ban" change at Welwyn Garden City school', *Welwyn Hatfield Times*, 20 March 2011

13. 'Obesity a "derogatory" word, says Nice', *Daily Telegraph*, 8 May 2012
14. 'Pre-surgery weight courses for obese patients criticised', BBC News, 5 July 2013
15. 'Volunteers who refuse CRB checks not welcome, Archbishop of Canterbury warns', *Daily Telegraph*, 24 July 2013
16. Testimony from Scout volunteer
17. People who work with children often self-police by asking themselves: 'How would what I am doing right now look to someone who was out to get me?'. *Don't Touch – The educational story of a panic*, Heather Piper and Ian Stronach, Routledge, 2008
18. Reverend Jeremy Hummerstone. The dossier also includes the fact that he posted a *Daily Telegraph* article on the church notice board which was critical of child-protection procedures.
19. A case of wardens hiding in bushes: 'Dog walker fined for taking pet into exclusion zone in Blaina despite warning signs having been stolen', Wales Online, 12 December 2012
20. 'Whistleblower: public misled on Islington's dog squad', *Islington Gazette*, 24 August 2012
21. Statement from Louise from Stoke on Trent, fined by Kingdom Security: *Litter fines – the corruption of punishment continues*, Manifesto Club Briefing Document, 27 December 2015
22. Interview with youth officer for the Peterborough Diocese, 2006
23. The exchange had been available on YouTube: http://www.youtube.com/watch?v=-UqM56e-kRA
24. 'Miniskirts ban in Italian resort', *Guardian*, 25 October 2010
25. *Checking Up*, Josie Appleton, Civitas, October 2014
26. *Authority: a Sociological History*, Frank Furedi, Cambridge University Press, 2013

27. 'Private security guards get yet more police powers', Manifesto Club Briefing Document, 5 July 2012
28. *The Audit Society*, Michael Power, Oxford University Press, 1999
29. Quoted in *Karl Marx's Theory of Revolution – The State and Bureaucracy*, Hal Draper, Monthly Review Press, 1977, p317
30. *The Origin of the Family, Private Property and the State*, Friedrich Engels, Junius Publications, 1994, p163–4
31. *The Making of Bourgeois Europe*, Colin Mooers, Verso, 1991
32. *18th Brumaire of Louis Bonaparte*, Karl Marx
33. *Karl Marx's theory of Revolution – The state and bureaucracy*, Hal Draper, Monthly Review Press, 1977, p468
34. *Nomenklatura: The Soviet Ruling Class*, MS Voslensky, Bodley Head, 1984. Also described in Leon Trotsky's *The Revolution Betrayed*
35. *Nomenklatura: The Soviet Ruling Class*, MS Voslensky, Bodley Head, 1984
36. 'Bureaucracy', in Economy and Society, Vol 2, Max Weber, University of California Press, 1978
37. *The British Regulatory State*, Michael Moran, Oxford University Press, 2003, p147; p92. Moran sees this as a largely positive development, as the rationalisation of the state and its subjection to clear and publicised rules, a welcome replacement of the closed world of the private club. He is correct about the deficits of the old system but overly positive about the new.
38. 'Une année au cœur de l'ENA', *Le Monde Magazine*, 22 October 2010
39. *Notre État: le livre-vérité de la fonction publique*, Robert Laffont, 2000
40. 'Orwell's war on the orthodoxies of left and right', Bruno Waterfield, *spiked*, 2 May 2014
41. The British financial market was regulated largely on the basis of people 'giving their word'. At a local level, interests

were mediated in a similarly informal manner, through social institutions such as the Rotary Club or Masonic lodge. Up until the 1970s planning decisions in the East End of London were made in the Masonic lodge, under whose roof gathered the police, union leaders, council representatives, business leaders and crime bosses. Weber gave England as an example of a country which had been 'incompletely bureaucratised', which retained elements of aristocratic culture in the organisation of its state.

42. *Banished: The New Social Control in Urban America*, Katherine Beckett and Steve Herbert, Oxford University Press, 2009

43. *L'Ancien Régime et la Révolution*, Alexis de Tocqueville, Folio, 1985

44. Officious rules, however, can never replace morality and codes in the regulation of civic life. As Max Weber noted, 'collective order' is 'only to a small extent the result of an orientation towards legal rules'. *Max Weber on Law in Economy and Society*, Harvard University Press, 1954

45. 'Hobby clubs: no under-18s allowed', Josie Appleton, *spiked*, 5 April 2007

46. *Leafleting – A Liberty Lost*, Josie Appleton, Manifesto Club, 29 July 2011

47. *Checking the Checks – Restoring Trust*, Manifesto Club report, 27 November 2015

48. The Disclosure and Barring Service, which performs criminal-records checks, is self-financing. Although it is linked to the Home Office, and receives some funding, it is run as an independent business.

49. 'Leader of Liberal Democrats on Lewes District Council attacks remarks', *Sussex Express*, 24 March 2014. The offending councillor had said: 'I believe that all business owners, Christian, Muslim, gay, straight, should be allowed to withhold their services from whomever they choose whenever they choose. It's their business. Why should they

be forced to serve or sell to anyone?'

50. *Don't Touch – The educational story of a panic*, Heather Piper and Ian Stronach, Routledge, 2008

51. 'Why do schools really stop parents taking photographs of their children?', Josie Appleton, *Guardian*, 23 June 2012

52. See for example Tinsley Park Golf Club's child protection policy: http://tinsleyparkgolfclub.co.uk/assets/files/Tinsley%20CIG%20Policy%2011%20website.pdf. The guidelines issue from sport governing bodies.

53. 'Police defend drowning death case', BBC News, 21 September 2007

54. There remained a few exceptions in 'public order' areas in Britain, such as theatre play licences and alcohol licences.

55. In Camden, London.

56. A quarter of UK authorities have 'free literature distribution licence' schemes. *Leafleting – A Liberty Lost*, Josie Appleton, Manifesto Club, 29 July 2011

57. See Licensed Royal Parks fitness operators: https://www.royalparks.org.uk/park-management/licences-and-permits/fitness-training-licences/licensed-royal-parks-fitness-operators

58. Birmingham City Council states: 'You are welcome to use our parks or green open spaces as backdrops for your wedding photographs and/or film recordings of your Wedding day for personal use only, with prior permission from us. Use service specific Parks form to make your request providing dates, times and the name of the site where you want to take your photographs. There is a charge of £265 for commercial photographs and £60 for non-commercial photographs.'

59. 'Council bans writers' pub performance', *Cambridge News*, 4 November 2008

60. For example, a group campaigning in Bromley South, quoted in *Leafleting – A Liberty Lost*, Josie Appleton,

Manifesto Club, 29 July 2011, p42
61. 'Why do schools really stop parents taking photographs of their children?', Josie Appleton, *Guardian*, 23 June 2012
62. 'Sex on campus', Brad Koffel, Koffel Law Firm blog, 8 November 2011
63. 'Consent conscious superkit' is available for purchase: http://consentgear.com/products/consent-kits-bracelets-consent-kits?channel=buy_button&referer=http%3A%2F%2Faffirmativeconsent.com%2F&variant=7547014657
64. Gloucester Cathedral
65. This was the argument used against Occupy London protesters outside St Paul's cathedral, London.
66. Councils including Woking and Swindon require risk assessments of all stalls, along with the measures taken to ameliorate this risk. *Leafleting – A Liberty Lost*, Josie Appleton, Manifesto Club, 29 July 2011
67. Woking Council requires insurance for leafleteers; Tameside Council requires insurance for those putting up posters. *Leafleting – A Liberty Lost*, Josie Appleton, Manifesto Club, 29 July 2011
68. This occurred at Belfast Exposed photography gallery, Belfast
69. This occurred in one Daventry village primary school
70. *The Audit Society*, Michael Power, OUP, 1999, p14
71. Ibid., p100
72. Ibid., p120
73. *Law and Marxism: A General Theory*, Evgeny Pashukanis, Pluto Press, 1989
74. 'China', in *Lectures on the Philosophy of History*, GWF Hegel, Dover Publications, 1956, p128; p126
75. 'Classrooms put under "permanent surveillance" by CCTV', *Daily Telegraph*, 20 April 2014
76. 'No terror arrests in 100,000 police counter-terror searches, figures show', *Guardian*, 28 October 2010

77. For example in the British Library in London. The search was introduced several years ago because of 'ongoing security concerns' and has been maintained.

78. 'School drug tests: Costly, ineffective, and more common than you think', *Washington Post*, 27 April 2015

79. 'Judge rules fingerprint jail security is unlawful', *Herald*, 17 March 2012

80. 'No fingerprints, no entry: Romford pubs introduce 'Orwellian' tactics to curb troublemakers', *Romford Recorder*, 21 February 2014. 'Human rights groups slam new fingerprint and ID scanning scheme for getting into pubs and clubs', *Your Local Guardian*, 16 February 2015

81. These were the Vetting and Barring database (for adults working with children), and the ContactPoint database (for children under 18).

82. *Leave Those Kids Alone: How Official Hate-Speech Regulation Interferes in School Life*, Adrian Hart, Manifesto Club, September 2011

83. *The Myth of Racist Kids*, Adrian Hart, Manifesto Club, October 2009

84. Conference about ContactPoint, 'Children: Over Surveilled, Under Protected', hosted by Professor Eileen Munro at London School of Economics, 27 June 2006

85. Lifestyle factors include 'poor problem solving/coping skills' or 'impulsive, chaotic and impulsive lifestyle': https://www.gov.uk/government/uploads/system/uploads/attachment_data/file/227649/dbs-barring-decision-process-sjp-template.pdf

86. *Students Under Watch*, Valerie Hartwich, Manifesto Club, September 2011

87. 'Locking artists out of the UK', Manick Govinda, *spiked*, 18 November 2013

88. 'Fingerprint scans for visitors at day nursery', *Bolton News*, 23 June 2010

89. 'School's Free Lunch Program Scans Students' Thumbprints, Sends Data To Government', HNGN, 20 June 2015

90. 'Critique of Hegel's Doctrine of the State', Karl Marx, *Early Writings*, Penguin, 1977, p108

91. *Checking the Checks – Restoring Trust*, Manifesto Club, 27 November 2015. Also cases cited in 'How the Child Protection Industry Stole Christmas', Manifesto Club, 20 December 2006

92. 'Football banning orders are out of control', *Guardian*, 17 June 2010

93. Incident communicated via email

94. 'Defend the Republic! Ban the burqa!', Josie Appleton, *spiked*, 19 May 2010

95. *The Division of Labour in Society*, Emile Durkheim, The Free Press, 1984, p39

96. 'Kissing banned at railway station', *Daily Telegraph*, 16 February 2009

97. 'Rome restricts La Dolce Vita', CNN, 12 August 2002

98. Under the Anti-Social Behaviour, Crime and Policing Act 2014, anti-social behaviour orders have now been replaced and extended by Community Protection Notices (an on-the-spot ASBO issued by council officials), civil injunctions (for the prevention of nuisance and annoyance), and Public Spaces Protection Orders (which allow councils to prohibit any activity they judge to have a 'detrimental effect' on the 'quality of life').

99. *Banished: The New Social Control in Urban America*, Katherine Beckett and Steve Herbert, Oxford University Press, 2009

100. Ibid.

101. Sexual Offences Act 2003, Part 1, Section 13: http://www. legislation.gov.uk/ukpga/2003/42/section/13

102. Interview with Professor Andrew Ashworth, All Soul's College, Oxford

103. *PSPOs: A Busybodies' Charter*, Josie Appleton, Manifesto

Club, 29 February

104. *The Collapse of American Criminal Justice*, William J Stuntz, Harvard University Press, 2011

105. *The Tyranny of Good Intentions*, Paul Craig Roberts and Lawrence M Stratton, Broadway, 2008

106. 'Police "horror" at 200-capacity gig licensing exemption', Live Music Forum, 16 October 2009

107. *Leafleting – A Liberty Lost*, Josie Appleton, Manifesto Club, 29 July 2011

108. *Pavement Injustice – Rise of on-the-spot fines*, Josie Appleton, Manifesto Club, March 2013

109. 'Increased fines for offensive language leave bad taste in mouths of critics', *Sydney Morning Herald*, 6 February 2014

110. *PSPOs: A Busybodies' Charter*, Manifesto Club, February 2015

111. Interviews with street drinkers at homeless drop-in centre in Islington.

112. Previous criminal laws have been derived from different principles, such as: the principle of compensation for loss, e.g. in Mesopotamia, where law showed little interest in intent (an accident and a murder were punished in the same way) and issued different compensation rates for homicide depending on the 'worth' of the deceased. Or, with Tudor treason law, the law was derived from the interests and will of the king, and represented a direct defence of his authority and the basis of his power, such that it was an offence to 'imagine' the death of the king.

113. *The Death of Common Sense: How Law is Suffocating America*, Philip K Howard, Random House Trade, May 2011

114. *Max Weber on Law in Economy and Society*, Harvard University Press, 1954, p56

115. *The Theory of Communicative Action, vol 1*, Jürgen Habermas, Heinemann, 1984, p255

116. *Law and Revolution: The Formation of the Western Legal Tradition*, vol 1, Harold J Berman, Harvard University Press,

1983, p38

117. 'Whistleblower: public misled on Islington's dog squad', *Islington Gazette*, 24 August 2012

118. *The Corruption of Punishment*, Josie Appleton, Manifesto Club, 31 October 2012

119. *The Tyranny of Good Intentions*, by Paul Craig Roberts and Lawrence M Stratton, Broadway, 2008

120. 'Prescot conmen posing as litter hit squad members to demand money', *Liverpool Echo*, 5 December 2012

121. 'Policing by numbers', *Police Magazine*, March 2007

122. 'Met sex crimes squad "pressured victims to drop rape claims"', *Daily Telegraph*, 26 February 2013

123. This point was made well in Onora O'Neill's 2002 Reith Lectures, *A Question of Trust*.

124. *The Revolution Betrayed*, Leon Trotsky, Dover Publications, 1984, p84

125. *The Structural Transformation of the Public Sphere*, Jürgen Habermas, MIT, 1991

126. 'Daredevils defy health and safety zealots by holding Cheese Rolling race', *Daily Mail*, 27 May 2013

127. 'Hardy bathers win right to swim unsupervised', *Guardian*, 27 April 2005

128. *A Letter Concerning Toleration*, John Locke, Dover, 2002, p144

129. *Magna Carta*, JC Holt, Cambridge University Press, 1965

Zero Books
CULTURE, SOCIETY & POLITICS

Contemporary culture has eliminated the concept and public figure of the intellectual. A cretinous anti-intellectualism presides, cheer-led by hacks in the pay of multinational corporations who reassure their bored readers that there is no need to rouse themselves from their stupor. Zer0 Books knows that another kind of discourse - intellectual without being academic, popular without being populist - is not only possible: it is already flourishing. Zer0 is convinced that in the unthinking, blandly consensual culture in which we live, critical and engaged theoretical reflection is more important than ever before.

If you have enjoyed this book, why not tell other readers by posting a review on your preferred book site. Recent bestsellers from Zero Books are:

In the Dust of This Planet
Horror of Philosophy vol. 1
Eugene Thacker

In the first of a series of three books on the Horror of Philosophy, In the Dust of This Planet offers the genre of horror as a way of thinking about the unthinkable.
Paperback: 978-1-84694-676-9 ebook: 978-1-78099-010-1

Capitalist Realism
Is there no alternative?
Mark Fisher

An analysis of the ways in which capitalism has presented itself as the only realistic political-economic system.
Paperback: 978-1-84694-317-1 ebook: 978-1-78099-734-6

Rebel Rebel
Chris O'Leary
David Bowie: every single song. Everything you want to know,
everything you didn't know.
Paperback: 978-1-78099-244-0 ebook: 978-1-78099-713-1

Cartographies of the Absolute
Alberto Toscano, Jeff Kinkle
An aesthetics of the economy for the twenty-first century.
Paperback: 978-1-78099-275-4 ebook: 978-1-78279-973-3

Malign Velocities
Accelerationism and Capitalism
Benjamin Noys
Long listed for the Bread and Roses Prize 2015, Malign
Velocities argues against the need for speed, tracking
acceleration as the symptom of the on-going crises of
capitalism.
Paperback: 978-1-78279-300-7 ebook: 978-1-78279-299-4

Meat Market
Female flesh under Capitalism
Laurie Penny
A feminist dissection of women's bodies as the fleshy fulcrum of
capitalist cannibalism, whereby women are both consumers and
consumed.
Paperback: 978-1-84694-521-2 ebook: 978-1-84694-782-7

Poor but Sexy
Culture Clashes in Europe East and West
Agata Pyzik
How the East stayed East and the West stayed West.
Paperback: 978-1-78099-394-2 ebook: 978-1-78099-395-9

Romeo and Juliet in Palestine
Teaching Under Occupation
Tom Sperlinger
Life in the West Bank, the nature of pedagogy and the role of a
university under occupation.
Paperback: 978-1-78279-637-4 ebook: 978-1-78279-636-7

Sweetening the Pill
or How we Got Hooked on Hormonal Birth Control
Holly Grigg-Spall
Has contraception liberated or oppressed women? *Sweetening
the Pill* breaks the silence on the dark side of hormonal
contraception.
Paperback: 978-1-78099-607-3 ebook: 978-1-78099-608-0

Why Are We The Good Guys?
Reclaiming your Mind from the Delusions of Propaganda
David Cromwell
A provocative challenge to the standard ideology that Western
power is a benevolent force in the world.
Paperback: 978-1-78099-365-2 ebook: 978-1-78099-366-9

Readers of ebooks can buy or view any of these bestsellers by
clicking on the live link in the title. Most titles are published in
paperback and as an ebook. Paperbacks are available in traditional
bookshops. Both print and ebook formats are available online.

Find more titles and sign up to our readers' newsletter at
http://www.johnhuntpublishing.com/culture-and-politics.
Follow us on Facebook at https://www.facebook.com/ZeroBooks
and Twitter at https://twitter.com/Zer0Books.